The thoughts of a mind locked in the Seventies

The WIT and WISDOM of BOLDNGREY

by Boldngrey

This edition first published in paperback by
Michael Terence Publishing in 2025
www.mtp.agency

ISBN 9781800949416

Cover Illustration
by Roy Carr

Cover Design
Michael Terence Publishing

Michael Terence
Publishing

Contents

Acknowledgements

I discovered how much I enjoy writing late in life and joined a small writing group as a retirement hobby. We meet weekly in Wimborne and discuss pieces that we have written. The shared interest in each other's writing has been a great encouragement. In consequence most of these pieces have come through that channel. I am grateful for the support I have received from all of our members. In particular, Nigel Harding has been a great help.

None of this would have been possible without John Jenkins, who runs our writing group. After a lifetime with the written word, he has been an inspiration and has led me along the way – teacher, mentor, critic, editor, and most of all, friend.

Two good friends have generously helped me with the artwork for this book. I am indebted to Jessamy Kiely for her superb illustrations and to Badg Champion for the excellent cover. Bob Limmer (Trim), kindly gave me permission to use his cartoon in Chapter 35. Their positive response to my pleas of poverty is much appreciated. The original cartoon on the front cover was done by Roy Carr.

I must also acknowledge the support of Mrs Boldngrey, more correctly known as Barbara, my wife of forty years. She has allowed me to pursue my scribblings untroubled for many evenings. She and other members of my family have listened patiently and, most encouragingly, laughed in the right places. Thank you.

Acknowledgements

These pieces have been written as a hobby and this book is not intended to make me rich. Any profits that may accrue will be given to military charities.

Preface

As a boy, I was fortunate to pass the Eleven Plus examination and go to a grammar school where I received an excellent education. However, at that time (1959), schools like mine were academic hothouses and had a very narrow curriculum with time for little outside of the examination syllabus. I enjoyed English lessons, but the creative aspect was a low priority, so I never learnt to enjoy just writing.

More than thirty years in the Army hardly improved matters as written work was always objective with adjectives only used with caution. I wasn't helped or encouraged when, on one occasion, my military writing was described as 'poor'. These days, I take that as a compliment.

After leaving the army, I suffered with post-traumatic stress largely as a result of events that I experienced in Northern Ireland in 1972. It took several years to get back on my feet.

In 2018, I wrote my autobiography, *Down Among the Weeds*. In part, it was a cathartic exercise. However, I found I enjoyed creating it, and, to my surprise, it interested some people and they enjoyed reading it.

Never one to worry about the position of carts and horses, I thought that having produced a book, perhaps I should learn how to write more betterly! I joined a local group of writers who meet each week. These pieces are a result. Some are fact, some are fiction, some are serious, and some are intended to be humorous.

Writing this book has been great fun and a happy exercise, releasing my stiff, chauvinistic mind, never cluttered by an excess of education, from its 1970s cave. I hope you will enjoy reading it as much as I have enjoyed writing it.

Either way, it's too late now 'cos I've got yer money!

(Boldngrey)

1

Rugby In My Blood

Until I was eleven, I was mad about football, but my traditional boys' grammar school played only rugby. To speak or even think of any other winter game was tantamount to treason.

Fortunately, I took to it with enthusiasm, played at county schools level, and was in the school's 1st XV from the age of fifteen. A couple of older friends were playing for Boscombe Down Rugby Club at weekends and told great tales of mischief. I tagged along, and a lifelong passion was born.

The attraction was the beer and the fact that it was a bit grown-up. I loved being part of such a disparate group. A few were quite good, a few were old stagers who once played well, but now dragged their bellies from scrum to scrum, and some were no-hopers who knew nothing of the game and were only there for the post-match revelry.

The opposition would be bought a couple of 2½ gallon jugs of beer. Then it was 'men behaving badly'. In the age before racism and misogyny and when 'gay' meant 'light-hearted and carefree', I was taught to sing by our forty-five-year-old, pot-bellied skipper. He would curse when the studs on his boots prevented him from treading on his last cigarette end in the car park as he sauntered onto the field.

At seventeen I played for Salisbury Thirds, fascinated by the antics of people who I had always regarded as respectable members of the community. Our family doctor was our fly-half. In his day he had been outstanding and played for London Hospitals. Sadly, his mind was still stuck in this era, but his body couldn't keep up. I would run alongside, calling.

'With you, Doctor Smith, with you', but he wouldn't see me as he was hopelessly short-sighted without his glasses.

He would shout 'Mine', charging forward with authority as the ball descended from on high. Then, with arms outstretched, it would land three feet in front of his myopic gaze and trundling opposition forwards would bury him.

Our captain was a highly respected local landowner who still farms along the A303 opposite Stonehenge. I well remember him one away game leading us to the bar and ordering 'Fifteen pints of throwing beer.' No prizes for guessing what happened with that.

Cadets at RMA Sandhurst were very fit, and the rugby was fast, hard, and serious. I loved it, and it provided an outlet for my occasional frustrations with the military syllabus. On Monday, I played for Blenheim Company; on Wednesday, I captained the Old College side; and on Saturday, I played for Camberley RFC. It was with Camberley that I once played at Twickenham. Not actually at 'HQ', but against the third team of Twickenham Rugby Club. 'When I played at Twickenham' is a line I would enjoy casually throwing out.

When the college rugby side went on a February half-term tour to Plymouth, the Saturday fixture was against Plymouth Argaum. The pitch was on the top of a wild and windswept hill on the edge of Dartmoor, so wet that the pink Devon mud squelched over your boots. We endured forty minutes of misery in a driving downpour. At the start of the second half, the ball hung in the wind and landed with a 'pludge' in the mud without bouncing. The ref called the captains together and we abandoned the match with the score at three all and headed for the clubhouse.

Argaum still had the old fifteen-man baths, which were just what was needed to warm us through. We were singing so heartily round the fire in the bar that we failed to notice the angry cries from Argaum Firsts when they came in cold, muddy, and miserable forty minutes later and discovered that we had used all the hot water and left them with baths of cold grey grime.

Back in Salisbury, I took the game more seriously. My debut for the Firsts was against Newbury, always a hard fixture My father came to watch, the first time he had ever seen me play. Newbury put the ball into the scrum. I was hooking and won it, to the delight of my chums and the fury of Newbury. At the next scrum, a fist came looping out of the dark depths of the Newbury second row, and I was laid out while pandemonium erupted. Unaware of the 'finer points' of the game, my angry ex-policeman father couldn't work out how his son had suffered such an assault. It was not just the first, but the only time he ever watched me play.

As bachelors in Germany, we had three main interests: playing rugby, drinking beer and chasing the local girls, some of whom were notoriously slow runners!

The regiment didn't play rugby, and we struggled to put out a team, which was deeply frustrating. Despite this, we always entered the competitions. We met our Waterloo against the Welsh Guards in the first round of the Army Rugby Cup. Our supporters numbered three. The Guards brought three coach loads, which reflected the size of our defeat - three points to eighty-three.

My opposite number that afternoon was Forty Evans, the regimental recalcitrant, who was only released from the Guard Room on match days. Despite the attention that Forty Evans had paid to my face, we still managed to celebrate the loss energetically. It became a long and eventful evening that ended with me being breathalysed by the German Police for riding a bicycle on the autobahn, probably a unique achievement and another long tale.

In my last season in Germany, I was selected to represent 2nd Armoured Division. I blinked as I entered the changing room. The team consisted of six members of the Welsh Guards, seven members of the Royal Regiment of Wales, a Royal Engineers officer (who was Welsh), and me. I know how Doctor Livingstone must have felt.

Very few of them seemed to have Christian names. Most were known by their last two Army numbers, as there were so many Joneses, Evanses, etc. Since we used numbers to identify our line-out moves and other set plays, we must have sounded like a demented bunch of code-breakers.

When I arrived in Poole, I became a rugby prostitute. I desperately wanted to play at a higher level at Salisbury, but the demands of the service meant that I couldn't guarantee regular availability. Consequently I always travelled with my boots in the car, hoping to bum a game if, as frequently happened, a team was short.

On Easter Monday, Salisbury was hosting a touring team from Old Shootershillians. Shoots were short of a player; so with my boots in the car, I ran out for them against my old friends.

On the last day of their tour, Shoots were suffering a massive collective hangover and were hammered by Salisbury. A festival of running rugby began with a try for Salisbury in the first few minutes. The sun shone brightly as the Salisbury conversion sailed over the bar and smashed a huge window in the new clubhouse that had been opened only that day.

Early in the second half, a ball bounced awkwardly over the Salisbury line. I sort of fell on it and scored one of the most memorable tries of my life. It was Shoots only score, and after the match, I was lionised as no Shootershillian before, presented with a tie and filled with beer all evening.

Somehow, I found my way home, but I decided to cut my losses with Salisbury and try my hand with Poole Rugby Club. The standard of Rugby at Poole was lower than at Salisbury, but it was great fun with echoes of my chaotic early days with Boscombe Down.

Our scrum-half was a school teacher with a pudding basin Beatles haircut created with kitchen scissors by his teacher wife who sported an original version. Their sons, aged four and six, wore similar, cut seemingly, with large pinking shears. On Saturday mornings he ran a gym club and was late for the coach taking us for a fixture on the Isle of Wight. We arrived in Portsmouth in time to see our ferry departing. Most of us were on our second pint when one of the Committee came in and announced.

'It's OK, lads. We've spoken to the opposition, and they're happy to delay the kick off so we can get the next ferry.'

We arrived at Sandown and Shanklin Rugby Club in the gathering December gloom and agreed to play forty minutes in the first half and as long as the light permitted in the second.

Our scrum-half's training shoes and rugby boots were made by the same company, so they had identical trim. In the rush for the coach, he had packed one rugby boot and one trainer. Fortunately, they were for opposite feet, but it meant he passed elegantly off his left foot but fell flat on his face when passing to his right.

The second half became steadily more chaotic in the failing light. It reached farce when our full-back kept chasing the attacking winger until they were lost in the darkness. He probably touched down two pitches away.

I don't remember the score, but I do remember we wowed the opposition with our rendition of 'Hi Ho' from Disney's 'Sleeping Beauty' with the Poole boys shuffling around the bar on our knees. Boy, we were funny.

Playing on the hard-baked grounds in Malta was very punishing. There were only three teams on the island: the Army, the Royal Marines, and the RAF.

One of our stars was Albert, our diminutive, bald-headed Padre. He laced his boots, took out his front teeth and became a merciless enforcer. 'Love thy neighbour as thyself' would be temporarily suspended in his brand of muscular Christianity.

We (the Army) had the best clubhouse with an unusual painted pattern on the ceiling. We also boasted one of the most unusual initiation ceremonies. The unsuspecting new boy would find someone pinning his arms to his body. His trousers would be quickly removed, and his backside would be covered with emulsion. He was then lifted, and an imprint of his buttocks would be left on the ceiling. No exceptions were made, and there were some quite senior bum prints up there. It was wise not to visit with wives or girlfriends.

Wherever I served, I always joined the local civilian rugby club as it provided a break from military life and a point of contact with the local community. When we got married our first house was on Shooters Hill, convenient walking distance from Askeans rugby ground. Askes combined a high standard of play with some of the best rugby mischief I was ever involved with.

We had a regular fixture with London New Zealand, whose ground at that time was in the shadow of the ivy-clad walls of the All-England Lawn Tennis Club at Wimbledon. Along with my boast of having played at Twickenham, I can also claim to have played at Wimbledon—rugby, that is.

Our Wednesday evening training focussed on a Haka that we intended to perform. It was based on 'Humpty Dumpty':

Hum-pity Dum-pity sat onna wahhh
Hum-pity Dum-pity haddda great fahhh

And so on…

Hand actions, etc, fit easily, and it works well. Try it! Unfortunately, it didn't impress the Kiwis and we were lucky to escape alive. Colonials have no sense of humour.

Askeans was an 'open' club, but still recruited largely from Aske's School, and each December, the club's 2nd XV would play a match against the school's 1st XV as a sort of recruiting event. On one occasion when I played, the captain of the 2nd XV played scrum-half against his seventeen-year-old son who was captain and fly-half for the school. Father and son became the club's 2nd XV half-back pairing in the New Year, providing a fitting finale for Dad to hang up his boots. I pointed this fine example to my new, young wife, little knowing how prophetic it might be.

Back in Germany, on my fortieth birthday, I played for HQ 3rd Division in an Army Cup match against 27 Regiment RA. A fresh-faced young officer from 27 Regiment, seemed to be particularly focused on bundling me around in the rucks and mauls. I paid little attention to it. After the match he came up to me in the bar and very politely said.

'Excuse me, sir. I believe you used to play with my father.'

His father was a very mean prop forward with whom I had played and drunk beer many years before. I suddenly felt my forty years.

I returned to Poole just after the Falklands conflict. This time, I turned out for Wimborne, but again, the demands of the service curtailed the number of games I could play.

It was an important Navy Cup match for Royal Marines Poole against HMS Sultan. We'd had the captain's pep talk and warmed up in the changing room. An embrocation-filled atmosphere had the blood roaring through the veins. We jogged outside and were confronted with the sight of a helicopter standing right in front of the posts.

'Typical bloody aircrew, can't be bothered to park on the proper dayglo-painted helipad, have to park on our sports field.'

The Fire Piquet told us the passengers would only be a few minutes.

We threw the ball around and waited until a group of important-looking people, headed by a batch of very senior Royal Marines officers, approached from behind some trees. At this point, we stood in a line, arms folded, staring them down like a team facing the Haka. Then, as they got into the aircraft, we noticed amongst them a diminutive lady with striking fair hair and blue eyes, who had been visiting, post-Falklands, from her office in Downing Street. Delaying the kick-off of a Navy Cup rugby match is a serious error, even for a Prime Minister!

My twilight rugby years were seriously interrupted when I was given a heart bypass at the age of forty-seven. My eventual recovery enabled me to continue at Wimborne Rugby Club, this time with the Veterans. I was one of three Vets who had intimate knowledge of our local cardiac departments.

Each Wednesday evening, we would play an uncompromising form of touch rugby. In the winter, it was under floodlights at the club and, in the summer, on the beach at Sandbanks. Of course, we undid the benefit of the strenuous exercise by drinking large quantities of beer afterwards. Throughout the season, we played matches about every three weeks against similar-styled teams. I loved the Vets, but games were becoming more difficult – ironically, not because of my heart, but because of arthritis.

Around this time, I also passed another Rugby milestone. That season, my youngest son was captaining his school's 1st XV at scrum-half. The last game of the season was against the Old Boys, for whom his elder brother was playing, so my wife and I went along to watch. Unknown to others, I had spoken to the games master.

At half-time, there was a substitution, and I came on to make a guest appearance at prop for the Old Boys. Fortunately, it was very muddy, and the pace of the game was slow, so I spent a happy forty minutes kicking my son's fingers when he came close to the scrum.

At the age of fifty-three, it was a fitting way to end. After, I reckon, thirty-five seasons, numerous military teams and more than ten civilian clubs, I could remind my long-suffering wife of the day, shortly after our wedding, when I played for Askeans and our captain played against his son.

Rupert McCall wrote:

From the first time that you laced a boot
And tightened every stud
That virus known as 'rugby.'
Has been living in your blood
When you dreamt it - when you played it
All the rest took second fiddle
Now you're standing on the sideline
But your heart's still in the middle

For twenty-five years, my son and I had season tickets for Bath Rugby until arthritis put paid to that as well. Now I'm just a sad old armchair fan reduced to reliving times past.

Writing this piece, I was shocked to learn that an old boy from my school, who is close to a full England cap, is the grandson of a chap I played with many times at Salisbury. Browsing the club website, I see that two rooms in the clubhouse and the new stand have been named in honour of three old teammates, now deceased.

Might I have one day been honoured similarly had I been able to stay on? The 'Boldngrey Urinal' is probably the best I could hope for and, some might say, 'the most appropriate.'

But what's this? Among Salisbury RFC's many teams, they list a 'Walking Rugby' team. Yes, really. 'Walking rugby is a non-contact game for those older or less able who want to retain an association with the sport.'

Now, there's a thing. Surely that 'association' must also involve beer? I never officially hung up my boots. They remain mud-caked somewhere in the back of my wardrobe, just in case.

Perhaps one last hurrah?

Just don't tell my wife.

2

How Was Your Day

Life has been good lately: spring sunshine and blue skies. Then, just when things were going well, a trip to A & E. My wife drove me in, chatting all the way to keep my mind off my chest pains. It shouldn't be too busy at 2pm on a Wednesday.

I checked in at reception. 'Can you tell me your name… and your date of birth… and the first line of your address…?'

Then, through the swing doors, I entered a long room with people seated against the walls. I sat down on a hard, flat seat with a wipe-clean surface.

I counted how many people there were in the room, some twitching manically with their digital devices, some nearing the NHS four-hour target waiting time staring glassy-eyed at the wall. Each one locked in a private misery, part Dante, mostly Hogarth. Occasionally they would all look up in helpless expectation. The Doors to Salvation, which stood at the end of the room, would swing open and a chosen one would enter or leave.

'Boldngrey.' A voice called.

I stood up, buoyed by the early attention, and was shown into an office. Behind the mask was a very camp individual, so thin that he would have struggled to get wet in a shower.

'Can you tell me your name… and your date of birth… and the first line of your address…?

He then proceeded to pose the same questions that the receptionist had asked.

'You can go back to the waiting room now.'

Deflated, I returned to Hogarth, re-took my seat and unwittingly assumed the gloomy posture of the others. I counted how many people there were in the room.

The Doors to Salvation crashed open. Out came a worried-looking lady pushing a sad old man in a wheelchair. We all looked up. She whispered to her friend.

'He can't stand up, and they want to X-ray his ankle as they think it might be broken, but they haven't even got a trolley for him.'

Why do people always whisper in doctors' waiting rooms?

Mercifully, my wife arrived. People budged up to give us seats together and we counted how many people there were in the room.

Opposite us were three girls, late teens, students, Goths? All were in black with pasty white faces and crimson lips. One had hair pulled into spikes as if she had stuffed her fingers in a three-pin socket. Opposite me, the girl wore huge, heavy tractor boots easily capable of controlling a JCB. Her black fishnet tights were designer ripped to reveal acres of milk-white flesh liberally blotched an inky blue, which, when new, might have been neat tattoos. An art student? She sketched endlessly on a pad with livid stick-on nails, so long that she could hardly hold her pencil to draw.

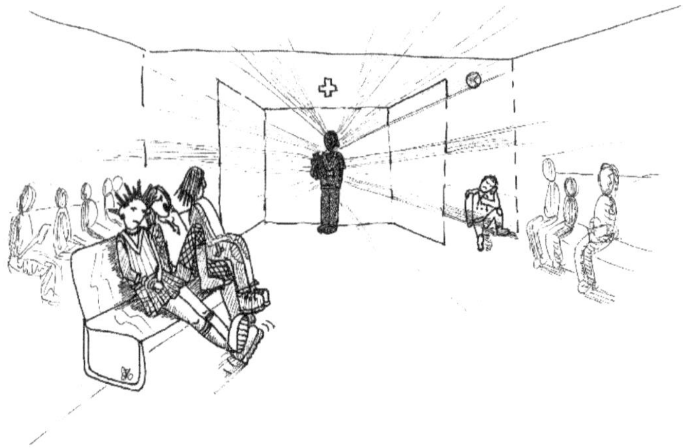

I counted how many people there were in the room.

Out through the Doors of Salvation shuffled a scruffy man, probably aged sixty, painfully thin, a shaven head and five days stubble. His mouth was sucked in where his teeth had once been. Dirty jeans ended three inches above dirty trainers. Clutched furtively in his hand was a freshly rolled ‘Old Holborn’ as he headed for the exit.

A younger couple arrived, both wearing stained tracksuits and trainers. The woman had her greasy hair dragged back in an ‘Essex facelift.’ Then she smiled to reveal a set of blackened teeth. Straight from Harry Enfield, it was Wayne and Waynetta Slob. They chatted animatedly and occasionally held hands.

‘Boldngrey.’

Framed in the Doors to Salvation stood an angel in blue. Wonderfully smart and efficient, probably Eastern European. Then, she got off to a bad start.

‘Can you tell me your name?’

I struggled to contain my inner Victor Meldrew.

'Yes, of course, I can tell you my bloody name. I've been able to do that since I was about three, and before you ask, I haven't moved house since I checked in at ten past two.'

I was shown into a blue-curtained bay and asked to lay on an examination bed, where I politely answered the rest of her questions.

'I'll need to take some blood.' she said, preparing the paraphernalia. I lay back and waited.

'Just a sharp scratch.'

No, it's not. It's nothing like a sharp scratch.

When are they going to revise the page in the Nursing Handbook that provides guidelines on what to say when taking blood?

'Would you like to return to Hogarth while we get this analysed?'

Head bowed, I trudged out through the Doors of Salvation and sat dejectedly with my wife. I counted how many people there were in the room, then showed her the cannula that had been neatly inserted in my elbow.

'Good omen, I reckon. They wouldn't do that if they didn't want to do more to me.'

'I've got one too.' the girl next to me said brightly. 'Looks like everyone has. A load of vampires in there, if you ask me.'

She was young and fresh faced with sandy hair – very sweet. Her name was Liz. So we filled a half hour cannula spotting: in the elbow, in the wrist, on the back of the hand, pink ones, green ones, yellow ones… It sure as hell beat counting how many people there were in the room.

The thin, scruffy man returned from his smoke break.

'… and now I'm on a litre of Vodka a day.' I heard him say to the man next to him. No surprises.

'Waynetta Slob.' She smiled at Wayne as she limped through the Doors of Salvation. Twenty minutes later she limped out just as I was finishing counting how many people there were in the room.

Wayne left the room, and the 'alky' departed for another smoke break.

'Liz.'

My friendly fellow traveller went in.

Wayne returned with two packages, and smiling together, they unwrapped them to reveal two jumbo junk burgers. They then proceeded to cram as much of the burgers into their faces as they could while chewing open-mouthed. They continued their animated conversation, oblivious to the quantity of detritus that they spat over the room. The smell of stale fried food was almost overpowering.

I was counting how many people there were… when suddenly there was a crash, and a man almost literally fell into the room. About forty, dirty and scruffy, head lolled on one side and probably high on something. He steadied himself and squinted at the wall, then fell against it and slid down onto a seat. He sat, eyes closed, head lolling towards a lovely lady next to him.

She squirmed with discomfort and tried to edge away. Each time he slid, she winced and shrunk further aside until, at last, she was forced to find another seat.

Liz came out, restored to health and wished me 'Good luck,' narrowly avoiding the outstretched legs of the junkie as she left the room.

'Boldngrey.'

My counting was again interrupted. This time, my optimism was tempered, and I passed through the Doors of Salvation, trying hard not to switch to full Victor Meldrew mode. The new cubicle had a phlebotomy chair, which, in terms of phobic provocation, is one step down from a dentist's chair and impossible to sit on comfortably. Somehow, I perched on an edge, and a new angel came in.

Neat and efficient as all the others, a doctor with an Irish lilt to her voice, a pretty girl with two rings in her nose and a ring in her lip. Why, oh why? Whatever happened to the neat clinical image of the senior members of the medical profession, but why should facial jewellery affect her professional ability? Was my mind stuck with Victor Meldrew in a nineties time warp?

'There's definitely a problem with your heart, so we want to do more tests on you. We're going to keep you overnight and probably send you on to the cardiology specialists tomorrow.'

The Doors to Salvation crashed open, and the junky stood there. Head cocked and wavering, he aimed at a chair, hit the wall and slid down onto the seat as before. A nurse saw him.

'Wake up… wake up… you mustn't go to sleep.' His eyes flickered open, and he mumbled. That was the only attention I saw him receive.

My wife was led in from Hogarth, and I was wheeled in a chair to the peace of an inner sanctum in the depths of the hospital. The next stage of my journey to the sunlit uplands of the Cardiology Department had begun.

Two days later, stented and restored by the cardiologists, I was able to return home to the spring sunshine and gaze again, untroubled, at the hills and blue skies.

***

The events and characters in this story are true with only slight embellishment. It illustrates the worst of the NHS, waiting in Accident and Emergency and the very best of the NHS in the speed and efficiency with which I was given life-saving surgery.

3

Serve To Lead

'Regard your soldiers as your children, and they will follow you into the deepest valleys; look upon them as your own beloved sons and they will stand by you even unto death.'

Sun Tzu, The Art of War

The Royal Military Academy Sandhurst, expresses Sun Tzu's principle in three simple words that adorn the cap badge of every officer cadet: 'Serve to Lead'.

This maxim recognises that the leader must always place the followers at the centre of all his actions. In my time at Sandhurst, Dan Fogarty was the embodiment of this.

Company Sergeant Major Dan Fogarty was a Coldstream Guard. He stood well over six feet tall, was very slim and wore his own particular version of a 'Clark Gable' moustache.

He was nearing the end of his twenty-two years' service and was not going to be promoted, so he had no need to impress the chain of command. He saw it as his role to turn the spotty youths of Blenheim Company into 'fine young officers'. His was the style of the Victorian father, fierce, dogmatic and with the ability to make our lives a complete misery, should he so choose; but despite our many shortcomings he was immensely proud of us and fiercely protective.

The working week at Sandhurst finished on Saturday morning with a drill parade by the whole Academy. In all there were about 1,200 men on the square, commanded by the Academy Adjutant, an Irish Guards Major, who sat imperiously astride a grey charger.

We had marched round the square numerous times and had satisfactorily completed the many drill movements demanded of us. The clock was approaching noon and we felt that we had done so satisfactorily.

The Adjutant, however, had a different opinion. From somewhere far in the distance, his voice rang out.

'Company Sergeant Major Fogarty, the third man in the front rank of Blenheim Company is idle. Take his name.'

Dan Fogarty snapped to attention and marched to the front of the company. Addressing no one in particular, with the staccato style of the Drill Sergeant, he bawled.

'YOU, SIRRR, MISTERRR, FISHNCHIPSIR, YOU'VE LOST YOUR NAME.'

He turned to his right and marched smartly back to his position. The ninety faces of Blenheim Company struggled to suppress a collective smile.

But the Adjutant was not going to be fooled by Dan Fogarty's top cover and repeated.

'NO, Company Sergeant Major, not MR FISH AND CHIP, the THIRD man in the FRONT RANK of Blenheim Company'.

Dan Fogarty marched to the front again and this time halted in front of the third man in the front rank.

'Mr Tupouto'a, sir, you're in The Book.'

On Monday morning, despite the best efforts of the Company Sergeant Major, Officer Cadet HRH Prince Tupouto'a of Tonga faced summary justice for 'failing to swing the left arm to the height of the breast pocket'. Later the same day, in another part of the Academy, I suspect that WOII (CSM) Fogarty D was formally interviewed by the Academy Sergeant Major.

For us, Dan could do no wrong.

4

The Red Button

Biden looked at the red button. He had made many mistakes, but starting the Third World War with a nuclear strike would be a 'BIGGIE'… 'Gee'. He felt tired. Perhaps he would have forty winks first…

He yawned and rubbed his eyes. Things went on in the world and folks got stupid, but it didn't matter. America sat at the top because he had that big red button.

He placed his chin on the desk and stared at its wonderful shape, round and smooth and sooo tactile. He ran his fingers round its base and the underside where it sat in the fitted interior of the briefcase. Sooo good. The fingers ran gently over the top and paused as he cupped them over the dome. It was his and with it, the world would dance to his tune. His eyes glinted with satisfaction.

His nap had refreshed him and flooded his mind with youthful playfulness. He gazed at the profusion of yellow lights beside it, each one with the name of a target alongside. Beijing, Moss-cow, Kabul, Montecito…

'Select yellow, press red' was the simple instruction that he had been given. If he pressed yellow and cancelled it with 're-set' nothing would happen.

Gee, those yellow buttons were so pretty and tempting, each one with a depression that neatly fitted the tip of a manicured finger.

He hovered, then stabbed a yellow. It lit up. 'Kinshasa! That'll teach those Congo boys.' He whooped with delight. He pressed another. 'Pyongyang! Ye ha! Take that, Fat Boy.' Then two more.

Klaxons blared in two missile silos in the Mojave Desert. Teams of men worked calmly, readying the missiles, wondering if this could be the last day of their lives. Similar things were happening among the giant redwoods of California.

He noticed the four lights made a square.

'That's purdy!' he thought and made another square. Four more weapons silos clicked efficiently into action. He pressed 're-set' then selected twelve that made a zig-zag pattern.

'Yay, just great.' He exclaimed in delight. Then he selected a pattern of pairs across the board.

Confusion ruled the Pentagon, and square-jawed men gazed at screens in disbelief. What the hell was going on? By now the Strategic Bomber Force was in two holding patterns over Alaska and Hawaii.

Was this World War Three? Who was attacking? From where?

The leaders of the most potent power in the world tried to figure it out. It seemed unlikely to be a real attack, but their cyber security had somehow been penetrated

Perhaps now they should wake the President from his 3pm nap.

Biden heard the footsteps approaching the door of the Oval Office and quickly re-set the buttons. He looked up from his papers as the Secretary of State entered.

'Mr President, we believe a foreign power has penetrated our strategic defence network.

'Oh, really…?'

5

The Serpent and The Kestrel

The ancient fortress had stood high on the cliff tops, proudly defending the city since the seventeenth century. For much of that time it had been a Royal Artillery garrison. The regiment currently occupying it consisted of four batteries, one of which was detached to support troops in Malta.

Gunner Steven Green was one of the soldiers serving in Malta. A quiet, unassuming young Afro-Caribbean, he was always known as 'Green S' as there were many other 'Greens' in the regiment. At eighteen years of age, he was a signaller in the Battery Command Post, where his task was to receive radio messages from the observers on the front and pass them to the command post staff. They would ensure that the guns fired quickly and effectively on the target. It was a job that required clarity and accuracy and, despite his youth, Green S was very good at it.

In their spare time most of the soldiers in the battery enjoyed an energetic duty-free lifestyle on the sun-kissed beaches of Malta, but Green was more introspective and, unknown to his mates, preferred to wander the cliff tops taking in the flora and fauna.

Green's star was rising and he was due to attend an advanced signallers' course in the UK, which would be an important step in his career progression. When he reported for his flight at RAF Luqa only the observant would have thought it strange that he was wearing a warm anorak on a sunny Malta day. After all, who knew what the weather might be like in England? On his arrival, he was not so lucky as a customs officer at RAF Lyneham *did* think it unusual and stopped him at the desk. At that moment there was a slight movement under Green S's jacket.

'Anything to declare?'

'No'

'Would you mind opening your anorak for me?'

As Green S opened his anorak a small snake fell out and wriggled on the floor.

The customs hall was thrown into chaos with people jumping and hiding to escape this killer reptile. Green S nonchalantly reached down and picked up his harmless pet snake.

'Stand there and don't let go of that snake while we get a box.'

The customs officer tried hard to retain authority and dignity. Someone brought a large plastic storage box which was too big and smooth for the curious little snake to escape from. Calm was restored and the snake assumed the identity of 'Exhibit A'.

'Pick up the box and come with me.'

Flanked by two customs officers, Green S was led into a back room of the hangar. He put the box on the counter and the events were described to a police officer.

'Right, lad, I'm arresting you on suspicion of bringing unauthorised livestock into the country. You're in trouble already so have you got anything else to declare?'

'Well, I suppose so.'

As he opened his coat a beautiful, young kestrel flew out and took a perch on the back of an office chair, where it assumed the identity of ‘Exhibit B’. Then, pausing only briefly, Exhibit B swooped into the storage box and seized Exhibit A behind the head before resuming its perch on the back of the chair. Exhibit A dangled lifelessly from Exhibit B’s sharp beak.

Green S quietly reached over and Exhibit B hopped happily on to his forearm. He removed Exhibit A from its beak and placed the deceased on the counter where, with order once again restored, it was labelled and placed in an evidence bag. By now an RSPCA officer had arrived so Green S gently coaxed Exhibit B into a cage and bade it a sad farewell.

Green S was then interviewed at length before eventually being sent on his way to the Royal School of Artillery to start his course. He passed with flying colours and was awarded an ‘Excellent’ grade. The original plan was for him to fly back to Malta a few days later and to spend the intervening time with the regiment. But he was pending civil trial, so a different fate was in store for him when he arrived at the Guard Room of the barracks. The broken-nosed Provost Sergeant greeted him and immediately threw him in a cell under ‘close arrest’.

The following morning, the Provost Sergeant marched Gunner Green S to appear before the Regimental Sergeant Major. The RSM was long, thin and exceptionally mean with an unrivalled talent for screaming obscene insults. In this case, he excelled, and in addressing Gunner Green S, he managed to cram the ‘F’ word as a noun, verb, adjective and adverb into just two short sentences. He formally released Green S from ‘close arrest’ into ‘open arrest’ and sent him to work in the Regimental Signals Stores until his court case was heard.

A few days later, in one of those inexplicable military ironies, the same RSM marched the same Gunner Green into the Commanding Officer’s office to be formally congratulated for an excellent report on his signals course.

Life in the Signals Store was a doddle and open arrest meant little more than being ‘gated’ within the barracks. Several weeks later his case was due to be heard. As usual, the list of Court cases was published and a number of reporters from the local papers attended. The normal custom on these occasions is for the soldier to be accompanied by an officer who would give a character reference in mitigation. Both soldier and officer are pressed and polished to perfection in order to make the best possible impression.

Green S pleaded ‘Guilty’ and expressed his regret and remorse. In mitigation, he said that he loved animals, often rescuing the young or distressed. His duty had taken him from Malta for several weeks and there was no one to take care of his pets while he was away. He just couldn’t bear to leave them. His humble and compassionate manner shone through and, of course, the officer was able to speak in glowing terms of his recent performance on the signals course.

The magistrate was won over and fined him £40.00. Gunner Green's honesty had been impressive and the local evening paper reported the unusual case.

The Adjutant sat in Regimental Head Quarters facing his usual mountainous 'IN' tray when the phone rang.

'Could I speak to Mr S Green, please?'

'I'm sorry, I'm not sure who you're referring to.

'Oh, I'm looking for, uh, Gunner Steven Green.

I'm from the BBC. I heard about his court appearance yesterday and we think it might make a nice human-interest story. Could we interview him, please?'

The Adjutant cautiously agreed and called the RSM as things needed handling carefully. The Army always takes a dim view of soldiers who break civil law as it brings the service into disrepute. On the other hand, Green's case was minor and could be good PR, so at 2pm, the Adjutant met the BBC team at the Guard Room, and Gunner Green S was produced. The RSM checked his dress and insured that his beret was set at just the right angle. He then stood behind Green just out of camera shot, ready to descend like a ton of bricks if he spoke out of turn.

Green S put in a starring performance with his quiet and honest manner. His compassion shone through as he told of the heart-breaking choice he faced of abandoning his pets in order to attend a career course. The historic buildings made an impressive backdrop. It was good TV and aired in the local evening news.

At eight thirty the following morning, the Adjutant was sipping his second cup of coffee when the phone rang.

'Hello, is that Mr Green, the man with the pets?'

'Uh, no, but I think I know who you mean. Can I help?'

'Well, I want you to tell him what a wonderful and kind young man he is, and I'm putting a cheque in the post for him this morning.'

'Thank you, that's most kind.'

He put the phone down and rubbed his chin. The phone rang again.

'What a fine young man that Mr Green is. If there were more people like him, the world would be a better place. Is it possible to make a donation?'

'Well, yes, I suppose you can if you send a cheque to this address made out to 'S Green'.'

The phone rang again and several more times. The messages were all similar and by the end of the morning Gunner Green S had pledges of around £150.00 from his admirers.

A week later Green S reported for his RAF flight back to Malta, his warm anorak zipped away in his suitcase in the hold of the aircraft.

He quietly took his seat and closed his eyes. For the two-hour flight his thoughts drifted away once more to the cliffs of Malta, to quietly wandering and finding other animals to take home. The sad loss of his two pets, Exhibits A and B, cushioned by the neat profit he had made from his court appearance.

6

Malcolm and Doreen

The advertising manager was cautious when he received the phone call from one of the country's leading dating sites. His was a nationally respected company established to serve the needs of the ageing population so it was an unusual and intriguing proposition. He quickly realised that a 'pensioners' portal' on a dating site could open a whole new customer base.

Malcolm was one such customer. Happily retired and single, he had nursed a lingering regret that the sexual liberation of the Swinging Sixties had somehow passed him by. Could this possibly be his one last chance?

He carefully crafted his profile with a picture cropped from an advert with a Marlborough man type of appeal, but somehow, his name didn't seem to fit. Malcolm was just a bit, well… Malcolm? Dirk seemed more rugged. Yes, Dirk it would be.

Doreen was quite taken by Dirk's post. Her profile picture was taken from her niece Harper's wedding photo. It was just head and shoulders as even she felt that 'petite and curvy' might be a little fanciful for her five feet tall and eleven stone figure. 'Sasha', she thought, was an alluring handle.

They exchanged several messages. Then, for a first date, Doreen suggested a rendezvous on the bench on the right as you entered the local park.

This was a bus ride for Malcolm so he prepared early. He treated himself to a new Gillette safety blade and concentrated on getting a clean shave. He winced from the sting of the Brut that his auntie had given him one Christmas in the Seventies. 'Splash it all over!' Henry Cooper had said, but not Malcolm. Oh no, far too precious for such extravagance, so it had lasted well.

The heavy cord trousers from Millets had loyally seen him through many important events, so he paired them once again with his trusty Hush Puppies. His journey would take him through the lunch hour, so he wrapped a sardine sandwich in greaseproof paper to get him through.

Gazing in the mirror, Doreen carefully painted her lips with a crimson cupid's bow and admired her hair that had been neatly set by Mavis-next-door. Her assignation with 'Dirk' had been just the excuse she needed to splash out on the new winter boots that had screamed at her from the shelves of Primark. Perhaps knee-high, black patent with thick platforms and vertiginous heels might be just a little adventurous?

Malcolm had eaten his sardine sandwich and sat checking his watch. Just a few minutes to go. Then a few minutes after. *Where was she?*

The walk in her new boots was more challenging than Doreen had expected so she was a little late when she arrived at the park gate. She peered cautiously over. A man was sitting on the bench on the right. It must be Dirk. The moustache was slightly more Alf Garnett than Burt Reynolds, but, yes, he was OK.

She clip-clopped awkwardly up to him and smiled revealing a small smudge of lipstick on her teeth.

'Hello, I'm Sasha. You must be Dirk'. In a Dietrich tone that owed its origin mostly to Woodbines.

He looked up from his watch and gasped in awe at the figure in front of him, barely able to contain his admiration. He brushed the crumbs of sardine sandwich from his pullover and nervously held out his hand.

'Hello. Yes I'm uh… Dirk. Pleased to meet you. Should we take a stroll along by the lake and perhaps we can have tea in the café?'

Doreen's heart fluttered as he cautiously clasped her hand. She squeezed his in response, all the while staring nervously ahead. They set off for the cafe, she, secretly hoping that it was not too far for her now painful feet and he, slightly worried that tea and cakes for two might edge into his bus fare home.

Together they shared a little cloud of happiness. The advertising manager had done a good job.

Alternative ending - PG.

They set off for the cafe, she, secretly hoping that it was not too far for her now painful feet and he, wondering if at last, he might get to use the Durex Featherlite he had bought so optimistically in 1973.

7

Three Hours In Belfast

He was standing by the loading bay inside the gate of the old warehouse that was now their home. Tall and slim, with three stripes on his arm he came from one of the hardest areas of Liverpool. His name was Graham Adams, but to everyone he was just 'Scouse'.

The eight men of the patrol were walking towards him in ones and twos, unsmiling, some taking a last drag from their cigarettes. Each one shuffled into the semicircle of sandbags, and fitted a magazine of ammunition to his weapon.

The sentry dragged the gate open and the patrol crashed out taking cover over an area of about thirty metres, making the task of possible snipers more difficult.

He led off along the main road before cutting abruptly between two houses and entering Livermore Avenue on the council estate.

A couple of kids, aged about ten or twelve, cycled up and down past them shouting insults. More joined in.

Other kids arrived, bigger kids. Several adults seemed to be directing things. The first stone was thrown from a flank and fell harmlessly, well away from the number three. A steady hail began, mostly small stuff that was easy to avoid. They stayed just beyond rubber bullet range.

A blue Austin Maxi was parked carelessly at the roadside. Scouse focused on it as he approached. The boot catch was missing. He stopped, held up his arm and went down on one knee. The patrol melted into cover and the stone throwers came closer.

He could see scratch marks round the place where the button catch on the boot had been. It was tied down with string. Breaking into a car and hot wiring it was easy, but to open the boot you needed a key. Stolen cars often had the boot forced open. It could be a bomb, but if the kids were still close, the chances were that it was safe.

He checked with Ops. 'Suspect stolen car. Austin Maxi, blue, number…'

A man scurried out of a house towards the car. Scouse stepped in his way. 'Is this your car, sir?'

'Bloody right it is and these kids are gonna wreck it because of youse British bastards.'

'Can I see your licence please, sir?'

The man was fumbling in his pocket when the radio opened up.

'Austin Maxi, blue, number… registered to Michael O'Brien of 27 Livermore Avenue, Belfast.'

'That's me, that's me, it's my bloody car!' He said thrusting his licence forward.

The name checked out and the photo just about matched. 'Thank you, sir. Be a good idea if you got an in-date tax disc, though.'

He scowled, snatched his licence back and roared away from the stone throwers.

They approached a sharp bend and the stone throwing intensified. The Adults came closer and the soldiers responded with rubber bullets.

They scored a hit and the patrol ran forward firing more rubber as friends dragged the victim away. The soldiers chased hard and a running battle ensued.

As they rounded the bend the kids seemed to disappear. On the right was a grassy area with swings and they realised they were caught in the open. There were two sharp cracks and bullets struck the roadside to the left of Gunner Bennet, the last man in the patrol.

He dived behind a low garden wall, panting hard and shaking uncontrollably. He struggled to gather his wits. Two houses away a bedroom window was opened flat to the wall. He snatched two quick shots at the black square and saw them hit the roof above. Two shots pinged off the path beside him in reply.

'Bastard, bastard! Breathe, for Chrissake, breathe!' He screamed at himself.

He took a long slow breath, held it, then slowly exhaled. As he breathed in again he tightened his grip and focused his aim on the window. He held his breath and squeezed off two rounds.

Scouse doubled back to the cover of a garage and made the 'on me' signal for the lads to join him. Benny was pinned down. The rest ran in and knelt in front of him, breathing heavily.

'Target is left-hand semi behind us. Dinger, you, Webby and Joe cut-off in the gardens behind. The rest through the door. Jimmy and Tom upstairs, the others with me. Any questions?'

He looked across at Benny with a thumbs up. Benny acknowledged. He pulled Bombardier 'Dinger' Bell to his side.

'OK… GO!' Dinger and his team ran forward in a crouch.

As they disappeared behind the house.

'With me… GO!' and they rushed the door with Benny giving covering fire at the window. The door gave easily. He charged into the living room, rifle in the shoulder, finger on the trigger…

Momentarily stunned, mind racing, he was pointing his weapon at a young woman holding a baby. Eyes wide and screaming hysterically, she was clutching the crying child to her cheek.

'Stand still, STAND STILL… Over against the wall.' He motioned.

It was all he could think of saying. He might have shot her. Heart pounding, he tried to be calm. 'OK, sit on the settee, but don't move a muscle.'

Sobbing, the woman complied. He knew her, Bernadette Dempsey, the tenant, husband Peter Dempsey lost an arm in an IRA bombing, currently interned. She was regularly stirring it up with the women when things happened in the estate. They had long suspected that this was a 'safe house'. Young and pretty meant nothing. She needed watching like a hawk.

'Don't let her move'. Two soldiers stood in front, staring at her in silence.

He moved into the hall and noticed through the kitchen that the back door was open. The gunman had fled. He took out his pocket radio. He'd called for back-up. Where the hell were they? Now he needed someone to care for that bloody woman.

The upstairs team reported. ‘All clear, Sarge. No blood, but Benny’s shifted a bit of plaster.’

‘Great, tell Dinger to come in.’

Two kids rushed into the house. ‘Where’s our mammy? Ye’ve got our mammy, ye English bastards.’

Twelve years old, but he spoke the language well.

‘Dinger, I’ll look after inside. Leave the lads at the back and you look after the front. Call Benny in to lend a hand. Things are starting to brew up out there. Tom, lock the front and back doors and stick with me for the moment while we sort these kids out.

‘Right, boys. I’m going to take you in to your mammy, but I want you to sit quietly with her on the sofa. OK?’

He opened the door and immediately lost control. The boys rushed in to hug their mother who stood up with the crying baby. The soldiers on guard stood in her way to stop her moving too far.

‘SIDDOWN! All of you sit down or I’ll take the kids out.’

With an arm round the younger boy, she obeyed.

‘You’ll not be happy ‘til you imprisoned all my family, ye bastard.’

The familiar whine of Saracen engines. Back-up had arrived. The crowd was now much bigger and welcomed them with volleys of bottles and stones. Women blew whistles and banged dustbin lids on the ground. Troop Commanders deployed the new arrivals in the gardens and pushed people back.

The Battery Commander had crashed out the whole Battery and now took control.

'Good to see you, sir'

'And you too, Sergeant Adams. You've done a great job. Quick update, please.'

'Right, sir, the gunman had gone when we lifted the house. Bernie Dempsey was in here with her baby. She's in the sitting room. I've had to let her two kids in with her or the crowd would have gone mad.'

His Troop Commander was on the BC's shoulder.

'Good kip, boss?'

'Piss off and get your hair cut Adams.' He smiled. 'Are the lads OK?'

'Yes, fine. Young Benny did a good job.'

Another Saracen drew up and two women got out, Corporals from the Royal Military Police.

'What've you got?'

'Bernadette Dempsey, Age 28, tenant, known sympathiser, suspected of harbouring a gunman. Oh, and she's got two kids and a baby with her.'

The RMPs grimaced at the mention of children.

'That'll make it difficult. Has she been arrested and searched?'

'Neither. All in a day's work.' Smiled Scouse.

'Are you Bernadette Cara Dempsey? Do you live here? I think you know the score. I'm going to have to pat you down before we take you for further questioning. If you stand with your hands on the wall, my friend will hold the baby.'

'You can piss off.' she screamed turning her back on the corporal. 'No one's taking my baby from me, not you bastards or anyone.'

'We're going to take you in, so it's got to be done somehow.'

It was stalemate. The tension was palpable.

The second corporal said calmly. 'How would it be if your son held the baby? She'd be quite happy with him and there will be no harm. It won't take a minute.'

After a pause, the elder boy took the baby and the woman scowled.

A scuffle was going on by the gate. A large middle-aged woman, red faced and angry was trying to push past the guard. The BC spoke to the Troop Commander dealing with the problem.

'What's happening, Richard?'

'Her name's Dempsey, sir. She says she's the woman's mother-in-law and wants to see the children.'

'The great British Army imprisoning women and kids – scum, the lot of youse.'

'With me please, Richard.' They went inside.

'We've got to find some way of dealing with the kids when we take Bernie in. If we bring her mother-in-law in and try and talk to her, she would be an ideal person to look after them. It's going to take very careful handling.' The Troop Commander nodded.

'I'll put a couple of chairs in the kitchen, sir.' Smiled Scouse. 'If it works we can keep her in there until we're ready to go.'

The BC nodded and went out.

'Hello, Mrs Dempsey, I'm in charge here. I wonder if you'd like to come inside and we can talk about Bernie and the children.'

'Talk, I'll give you talk. I've plenty to say to you…' She spat a string of expletives then shrugged past the man on the gate and was led to the kitchen.

'Take a seat Mrs Dempsey.' She sat down, arms folded, and he joined her. 'Do you live near here?'

'Aye, over the road at number 42.'

'That's good, it must mean you see a lot of the grand-kids.'

'Aye and see too much of you English bastards as well.'

'They're lovely kids.' He said, biting his tongue. 'You must be very proud of them.'

'Aye, good Republicans the lot of them.'

'Mrs Dempsey, you know that Bernie was in the house this morning when a gunman fired from the bedroom window. We're going to have to take her in and ask her some questions.'

'Bloody lies. You're making it up.'

'There's no question about it, Mrs Dempsey. We're taking her in and the children need you to look after them. Will you take them with you?'

Silence. Then a look that seemed to mean consent.

'Right, we'll let the kids say 'good bye' then take her to the vehicle. You can wait in here.'

A nod. They left her in the kitchen with a soldier and closed the door.

'We need to get out as soon as possible. Richard, I want two Sarries, prisoner and escorts in the first, a section in the second. I want an avenue of troops, arms linked, between the house and the first Sarry. There'll be a hell of a crush.

Sergeant Adams, tell the corporals, I want her wrists zip-tied and one on each arm to push and pull her through. Quite clear?'

'Clear sir.'

Back in the lounge. 'Right boys, your mammy's coming with us, but your gran's in the kitchen and she's going to look after you. Can you take the baby again?'

The kids howled and clutched at their mother. The writing was on the wall so she pushed them away.

'Go on, granny will look after you. I'll be OK.'

They were led away to their grandma, crying. Outside, the troops were forming up and the crowd's anger was rising.

Bernie's hands were zip-tied as ordered. The BC checked that everyone was ready and knew their tasks.

'Richard, ready outside?

'Yes, sir.'

The two corporals took Bernie to the front door and rushed her to the gate, the crowd baying and pressing forward. They squeezed between the two rows of troops, hands reaching through to grab her.

Suddenly they lost momentum. A hand had gripped her shirt and more hands held other parts of her clothing. The crowd was pulling her away from the soldiers and they were in danger of losing her. They frantically prized at fingers, beat hands and stamped on toes, anything to keep her moving. She was eventually bundled into the Saracen and the two vehicles drove off.

***

The Battery Sergeant Major was by the loading bay as the vehicles returned. He watched them go through their 'unload' drills and gave each NCO his next task. It was military banter and a pat on the back whenever he could.

Barely eighteen and eight stone soaking wet, Gunner Bennet was the youngest man in the battery.

'Hey Benny, my little hero. You did a great job there, son.'

'Thank you, sir.'

Scouse's patrol went straight to the Int Cell where they were debriefed. Cigarette smoke wafted through the door to the Ops Room.

Phone in hand, the watch keeper looked round.

'They've interviewed Bernie and had to let her go. Her swabs were clear and she said she'd just come back to the house and didn't know there was anyone upstairs. Nothing they could prove.'

No surprises.

Scouse walked to the accommodation with Bombardier Bell.

'Plucky little sod, Benny.'

'Yeah, I always thought so.'

'Just keep an eye on him. That was a hell of a thing he went through today.'

Scouse and the Troop Commander, Lieutenant Richard Balshaw, shared a sleeping area. He threw his weapon and webbing on his bed and sat down heavily. Head in hands he stared at the floor.

'Difficult day?'

Scouse accepted the invitation to talk. They had no secrets.

'No shit, Sherlock. I got suckered and nearly got Benny killed.'

'No, that can happen to any of us. I've done it, remember that day in Parkside?'

'Yeah, certainly do.'

He stripped his weapon and began cleaning it in silence. He looked up.

'That's not all, though.'

'I guessed not. What's on your mind?'

'I went through that bloody door, butt in the shoulder, finger on the trigger. I could have killed that stupid woman.'

'But you didn't. We've all done it. Don't beat yourself up about it. She should never have been there.'

'Yeah, I know. Thanks, Boss.'

It wasn't just Benny who needed watching. It was a hell of a thing that he went through that day.

Tomorrow they would do it all again.

8

Cars That I Have Known

My father was a police driving instructor, but cars and me just didn't get on. I became one of his greatest failures. With white knuckles gripping the steering wheel of his treasured Ford Anglia, I would drive nervously through the lanes of Wiltshire dreading the crunch of gears that would provoke another exasperated outburst.

I left home at seventeen and after a year as a Gunner and two years at Sandhurst, I was still unable to drive, but I did have the tweed cap and string-backed gloves! From the Royal Artillery Young Officers course I was due to go to a regiment equipped with Abbot, a 105mm gun mounted on a tracked chassis, so a major part of the course involved learning how to drive and maintain this equipment. Consequently, when I joined my first regiment in Germany, I was licenced to drive a full-blown tracked vehicle despite not holding a UK driving licence!

During my first summer, I spent eight weeks in Scotland with a recruiting team from the regiment. Four of us had a Land Rover and would tour the area visiting schools and Cadet Units.

With 'L' plates on the vehicle, I drove under instruction for most of the time. When the Staff Sergeant from HQ Scotland who was going to test me opened the passenger door of the vehicle he blinked as he was confronted by the steering wheel. Our German Land Rover was left-hand drive.

I'm not sure that he properly recovered from the shock, but somehow, I passed the test.

Back in Germany, one of my mates was selling his 1959 Morris Minor. For a year or more this trusty old vehicle carried me around including a couple of trips to the UK and back. I can't remember how it died, but I sold it for scrap to a cavalry regiment, who wanted to use it to accommodate the disco for their officers' mess summer ball. I didn't ask why.

My next posting saw me based at the Welsh seaside resort of Tywyn. I had been talking to a friend about buying a new car and, without too much thought, I said that I fancied zooming round North Wales in a Beach Buggy, 'Baywatch' style, all white teeth and California smiles. Unfortunately, I couldn't afford the real thing as the insurance would be prohibitive. 'Really? My brother can sort that out,' he said.

Sure enough his brother negotiated the purchase of an electric blue Beach Buggy, together with suitably worded insurance cover.

The Buggy was a standard VW Beetle chassis, but the body had been replaced with a low-slung fibreglass shell with fat tyres, bucket seats and a tiny twelve-inch steering wheel.

The exhaust system had been stripped and replaced with two motorcycle mufflers, which gave it a wonderfully throaty roar. The downside to this sporty sound was that Beetle engines are air-cooled and the part of the exhaust that had been removed was integral to the cooling system. If I cruised at more than 50mph, the engine overheated and squirted the oil all over the road. In the twelve months that I owned the car, I had three new engines; not actually new, as they cost about £50 each from the scrapyard.

The Buggy had no heater and a flimsy hood pop-fastened to the windscreen in a way that allowed the wind to whistle straight through.

Somehow, I had failed to appreciate that the weather in North Wales was totally different from California. There was just a brief spell in summer when the Beach Buggy became a prize 'babe magnet'. Everyone wanted to ride in it, but, sadly, only once.

It also had a problem with the starter that I never quite got to grips with, mainly because it was very easy to bump start. Consequently, I spent much of my time looking for a girlfriend who was strong enough to push my car in high heels. Unfortunately, those in North Wales who fitted the bill could usually carry a sheep under each arm and fell short in several other important criteria.

I gave up with the buggy at the start of my second winter and replaced it with an old Mini Van which was far more practical, but only slightly more reliable. In this case the problem was with the braking system. When you pressed hard on the brake pedal, it continued to go down to the floor as brake fluid seemingly escaped through one of the seals. Again, I never quite got to grips with the problem, as I found that you could just kept topping up the brake fluid. (Don't try this at home, kids.) Asked about the van, I would say. 'It does forty miles to the gallon and sixty miles to a can of brake fluid.'

When I left Wales, I replaced the Mini Van with a Mini Traveller with the wooden side trim.

In 1976, I was sent on an operational tour to Oman. Jobs like this, with nothing to spend your money on, are a great opportunity to save, provided you don't mind being shot at from time to time. I came home with a big bag of gold, with which I bought a wonderful Triumph GT6.

The GT6 was based on the Triumph Spitfire body with a 2,000cc V6 engine. It was seriously nippy and enabled me to bring danger to roads all over Britain. Sadly, I sold it before my next posting to Malta. It was probably the best car I ever owned. These days similar vintage models are fetching more than £30,000.

In Malta I found a lovely, little cherry-red Austin-Healey 'Frogeye' Sprite. With sunshine from May to October, it had the 'babe magnetism' that the Buggy lacked. It soon attracted the girl who was to become my wife.

My mistake was to ship it home when I left Malta as its age caused constant problems (the car not the girl) and I would regularly break down on the motorway. Almost always the fault was a component that cost very little, but the unreliability meant it had to go. Newly-married, I replaced it with a boring Mini1000.

We were living back in Tywyn when our first child arrived, so the mini was replaced by a VW Golf, bought because of VW's reputation for strength and reliability. Unfortunately, the early models like mine had terrible problems with rust and in no time, filler was falling out of bodged repairs. One of the few times that I felt I got the better of a car dealer was when I traded it in for a Mondeo Estate. I had to hold the driver's door open very carefully while the dealer checked inside as the bottom door hinge had rusted right out of the frame!

Returning to Germany for my next job, I left the family at home for a few weeks to complete the school term. My plan was to take over the job and the new married quarter, then return home in the Mondeo, pack up the house in the UK and drive the family out.

The Mondeo had done us well and driving back I was careful to rest in accordance with all the recommendations. I was in a 50mph traffic jam about where the M27 becomes the A31. I blinked and at that moment realised that the traffic in front had stopped. I hit the rear of a Volvo - hard.

The rear bumper of the Volvo was a couple of inches higher than the front bumper of the Mondeo so the front of the Mondeo was pushed right back in a square shape to match the bumper of the Volvo which was virtually unharmed. I would have smiled had I not been crying so much. I arrived home courtesy of the AA sitting in the Mondeo on the back of a low loader.

With no means of getting to Germany to start our new life, the Boldngrey family went into panic mode, but strange things come from unusual circumstances. The car was comprehensively insured and was now with the local Ford agent who was able to do the repairs, but this would take weeks and I only had a fortnight's leave.

Nimble footwork by me and the Ford garage produced a remarkable result. The Ford dealer was prepared to take my car in part exchange for another second-hand Mondeo that I could have immediately. He could charge for the work needed on my old car to my insurance company through my comprehensive cover. The result was that the Boldngrey family arrived in Germany on time in a Mondeo Estate which was a newer, superior model to my original. Boldngrey one, motor insurance nil!

My next job was in Norway, a country that I had visited several times on military exercises, so I had an awareness of the hazards of winter driving. I also had in mind the practical demonstration, given on the M27, of the comparative robustness of a Ford Mondeo and a Volvo.

A Volvo 740 Estate saw us through three years in Norway and kept me safe on the three occasions when I left the road in winter. Just before we left Norway, I replaced it with a beautiful new Volvo 940 Estate.

A few weeks before coming home, I was driving up to Lillehammer. It was a cold, bright day, the road was straight, dry and empty. Eric Clapton was blasting 'Layla' just below the threshold of pain, and I was nearing the end of my journey. All was well with the world and I just let the Volvo run. Then, too late, I noticed a police car parked on the side of the road and a couple of kilometres later I was waved down.

It was all very complicated. My car was registered in the UK, but I told them that I was a British serviceman living in Norway. My unit existed in Norway under a unique agreement which was not secret, but was not well known.

There weren't any British armed forces in Norway so the policeman phoned 'the office' for advice.

It seemed that in Norway there was a sliding scale of fines for speeding which rose every 10kph that you drove above the national speed limit of 80kph. The last step was at 110kph, above which your licence was confiscated on the spot. Thanks to Eric Clapton I had been clocked at 113kph (about 70mph) and the police wanted to take my licence, then and there.

I was seriously worried and suggested that they could not take my British licence off me as I was returning to the UK permanently in three weeks' time and I would be unable to drive there. Things were looking bad and there were more confused conversations with 'the office'.

Desperately trying to be polite and helpful, I suggested that if, perhaps, they recorded my speed at 109kph rather than 113kph I could be given the maximum fine and we would avoid further complications. They rubbed their chins, 'the office' agreed and they awarded me an eye-watering spot fine of 3,000 Krone, more than £300.

I didn't know whether to laugh or cry as I was given a slip of paper to pay at a Post Office within seven days. I drove cautiously away consigning Eric Clapton to the glove box.

Shortly after, I returned home for good with the Volvo stacked with duty free alcohol bought through the service system. I was cautiously optimistic that the duty to pay would be reasonable, but with UK customs you can never be sure.

At Dover, the Customs Inspector approached me, a second officer by his side.

'You've come through the Red Chanel, sir. That means you have something to declare.'

'Yes, the car. I bought it tax free through the Armed Forces system.'

'Right, sir, if you come inside with your documents… John, here, is a trainee and I'm showing him the ropes. Have you got your…?'

I handed over a document. He checked it and explained it to John.

'And your…'

He did the same again and with my other documents. Thankfully everything was in order

'That's it, sir, all done. You can go.'

'I can go?' Eyebrows raised quizzically.

'Yes, sir, all in order. Enjoy your Christmas.'

I wasn't invited to declare anything else so my family enjoyed a pleasant duty-free glug due to an inefficient, or was it a kindly, Customs Inspector?

I kept the Volvo for 195,000 miles, always having it dealer serviced in the hope that it would retain some second-hand value. When the time came to sell it, I was saddened to get only slightly less for the Volvo dog guard and roof rack, which I sold separately, than for the car itself.

In retirement I've settled with a Citroen Berlingo. After a lifetime as a below average driver I'm happy in the slow lane with something that gets me from A to B in a safe and reliable manner.

Clarkson and his petrol heads can leave me in the dust.

9

Crash and Bang

'Crash' Self was a big man in every sense of the word, standing six feet tall, broad in the shoulder and, now in his late thirties, wide in the waist. Wherever you were on the gun position, there was no mistaking his broad Somerset burr. He was our Battery Sergeant Major and was one of those larger-than-life characters who regularly feature in the Army.

Crash would tell us that he had joined Two Eight Battery, straight out of training, as a seventeen-year-old 'long before the Dead Sea even went sick'. In the space of about nineteen years, he had risen steadily through the ranks to become the Battery Sergeant Major. Crash wasn't *in* Two Eight Battery; Crash *was* Two Eight Battery – nothing more, nothing less.

No one seemed to know how he got the nickname (his name was actually Colin), but, having travelled back in his car with him after away rugby matches, it could well have been because of his driving!

I remember after one away match, in the days before breath tests, Crash looking at one of the passengers and saying, not entirely in jest. 'You drive; you're too drunk to sing.'

Crash had a particular problem with the names of the four or five soldiers in the Battery whose parents had fled from Eastern Europe in the early fifties, Poles with surnames spelt without vowels. His solution was to call them all

'Smith' and add the first letter of their name: Grocowski, for example, became Smith G, Peplinski was Smith P and so on.

My favourite story about Crash is of one exercise when the battery was deploying to a new gun position. We had driven through the night and everyone was tired, but, on such occasions speed, efficiency and silence remain as vital as ever, with every member of the battery understanding his role and moving from one job to the next without prompting.

A key task was to establish radio communications as quickly as possible, with the principal radio set connected to an aerial on top of a twenty-seven-foot-high telescopic mast. Lance Bombardier Vic Jones's was ready to erect this mast, a job which two men could do with difficulty, but was normally done by four.

Jones looked round in the darkness for assistance, but the others were still busy so he took the kit and carefully laid it out. Still, no one was available so he fixed the base plate down and lugged the heavy mast into position. Telescoped down into its bottom section, it was about four inches in diameter, four feet long and heavy. He fitted the guys, but no one came forward, so he raised the first section and screwed the locking collar down. Then the second section, the third and so on, all the while waiting for assistance which never came.

With each section the load became heavier and the task more awkward as it began to sway in the breeze. But still no help came so he struggled on. He reached the final section and, with a mighty heave, he raised it to the full twenty-seven feet. Then disaster struck. One of the collars came unlocked and the whole mast collapsed with a resounding clatter, section by section down into the telescope. It was so loud that we all stopped and looked up expecting to see Jones standing beside a pile of severed fingers.

Crash sized up the situation immediately. No one was hurt and Jones had been doing the wrong thing for the right reason. He strode across, put his face inches from the hapless Jones and growled,

'Ere, lad. What does your village do for an idiot now you've joined the Army?'

Then he looked at the others, who stood by, smiling, and added,

'And you three, get over here and lend Jonesy a hand.'

Crash's biggest strength was his understanding of his men. He always knew where to find the loafers, but he would also spot the soldier who hadn't had a letter from home for a while and just keep an eye on him. Touchy-feely hadn't been invented in those days, but Crash was the bluff old uncle they could always rely on and they thought the world of him.

In Belfast, the admin staff were his particular responsibility and he was keen that they should always feel as important as the rifle troops. He saw it as essential that they were able to write home with exciting tales. 'Went on patrol with the BSM and picked up a couple on the wanted list' was much better than 'Worked hard in the stores all day getting things ready for the others.' It gave them a greater sense of purpose and the chance to tell a real 'war' story when they got home. They weren't to know, but he usually took them out on patrol at the lower-risk time of day, and, strangely enough, he often got results. His imposing figure was enough to impress the locals, oblivious to the fact that behind him in the patrol were two cooks, a clerk, two drivers and a nervous store man.

***

The twenty-sixth of September was just another Belfast day. At about 2230, I took a four-man patrol into the Riverdale Estate, wondering who we might find on their way home from the pub. As we approached number 25 Riverdale Park South, we noticed that all the lights were on and two men were standing at the garden gate, chatting and looking around suspiciously. They were dickers, sentries keeping watch for some purpose. They identified themselves and were both on our list of minor suspects.

Loud Irish music was coming from inside the house and we reckoned about thirty people were enjoying a rip-roaring party, so I reported it to Ops. I wanted to lift the house, but to do so with so many people inside would have taken time to organise.

The Battery Commander instructed us to go to the rear of the house and observe. As we looked back, people were already beginning to leave, alarmed by our presence. I was angry and frustrated as I thought we were losing valuable suspects. There was nothing that we could do about it, so we doubled back through the gardens to number 25.

I settled the lads into cover then found the biggest, blackest shrub in which to hide myself. I shuffled in backwards and was resigned to a long and, probably fruitless, wait. As I settled, I sensed the overwhelming smell of almonds and the membranes in my nostrils tightened with a familiar oily vapour.

It was unmistakable. I edged out gingerly, whistled to get Gunner Collins' attention and beckoned him over to me. I drew back the foliage and made a sniffing noise. Collins got the message, did the same and stepped back in surprise. 'Bloody hell, boss!' We moved away swiftly. The smell was unmistakable. I had discovered a huge cache of homemade explosive.

I radioed back to Ops and the Battery Commander crashed out the whole Battery. Unfortunately most people had left the house in the short time that it took for them to arrive. The bomb disposal officer (always known as 'Felix') brought with him a sniffer dog and his handler. While 'Felix' went straight to the bomb and set about checking the surrounding area for signs of explosives, the dog visited just about every dustbin, watered every shrub and found every cat scent in the street, but showed little interest. In short, he was the big, docile, settee-filling type of Labrador, not the smart weapon finder that we had hoped for. Eventually his handler drew back the foliage and almost put his nose on the cache before he finally showed any interest.

Inside were the tenant and three other people, one of whom was a short, skinny individual with heavy glasses. He bore a passing resemblance to 'Freddie' of Freddie and the Dreamers and was on our wanted list as a low-level activist. We sat the four on chairs in the lounge as the property was searched. Freddie was noticeably nervous and sweating.

The Troop Sergeant had spotted this earlier as he passed through. When he came back, he stopped dramatically in the doorway then came over to me and in a poor imitation of a stage whisper, said,

'Hey boss. That bloke over there – that's Freddie.'

Freddie looked over his shoulder, anxious at having been recognised. Then a few minutes later, from behind the closed door to the kitchen, a different voice shouted,

'Hey fellas, have you heard? They've got Freddie in there.'

Freddie began visibly shaking.

Shortly after, Crash came through the lounge. He stopped in his tracks in mock surprise, walked over to the man and said with relish.

'Well, well, well, Freddie, we've been looking for you for ages.'

This was almost too much for him and, by the time we got him in the Saracen to take him away, we could hardly stop him talking.

Outside, Felix had examined the find as thoroughly as he could among the dark foliage.

'I can't see much and I don't want to disturb anything in case it's booby-trapped. What's the area like?'

'Ninety-nine per cent hostile.' I replied.

'I'd prefer not to take any risks and blow it '*in situ*'. What do you think?'

'Delighted.' I replied and walked off to clear it with the Battery Commander.

The time for detonation was 0400 and, as Felix set about laying his charges, we went around the area knocking people up in the nearby houses. We had found a bomb, which must be detonated on the spot and they were asked to come out of their houses into the street to avoid any flying glass.

A small group of women, the usual suspects, moved among the houses carefully explaining that it was the 'Prods' who had planted a bomb behind Teresa's house. When we were sure that everyone was safe, at precisely 0400, Felix touched the terminals. There was an almighty bang followed by moans and gasps of horror from the locals and stifled sniggers from the soldiers. There was structural damage to some of the buildings, tiles were blown off the roofs, ceilings were cracked and windows were blown out all around. In the garden the bomb left a crater six feet round and three feet deep.

We had been out since 2230 and I felt our job was done, so I asked the Battery Commander if my little patrol could return to Casement Park.

Despite the breaking dawn, there was a spring in the step and a smile on our faces as we moved past the blast-damaged houses to egg banjos and a large mug of sweet tea in the cookhouse.

When the others returned, still full of adrenalin from the night's work, spirits were soaring. We all gathered for breakfast laughing and retelling events.

We had not been impressed by the sniffer dog and as usual Crash provided the most memorable comment.

'That bloody sniffer dog.' he said. 'I reckon Boldngrey could do a better job finding explosives with his backside than that dog does with his nose!'

Except, of course, he didn't use the word 'backside'.

10

Tea Without Sugar

Note: In the Household Cavalry a Sergeant is known as a Corporal of Horse

Arthur Beasley wore a small, toothbrush moustache, which first graced his upper lip in the late Sixties when it drooped past the corners of his mouth in the Zapata style made fashionable by the Beatles. On graduation, Arthur worked for a provincial law firm, where the moustache assumed a style more fitting to the profession.

Settled in his employment he proposed to Josephine, his university sweetheart, and they bought their first house near Guildford. Josephine (not Jo or, heaven forbid, Josie) steadfastly supported Arthur as he rose past the markers that indicate suburban success: a leafy Surrey home with a shiny black Mercedes in the garage, a *pied a terre* in London, president of his Golf Club and a Rotarian. They now enjoyed a busy retirement, but their one unspoken sadness was that they had no family. Children had simply not come along.

To make up for this Josephine had lavished her affections on a succession of small, fluffy dogs.

Arthur was resigned to not having children, but secretly hated these irritating little rugrats. The present favourite was Sugar, a small, yappy Pekinese, brushed and combed to such perfection that it was hard to tell which end was the head until you offered him a biscuit.

Arthur and Josephine Beasley were enjoying a few days in their London flat and on a bright spring afternoon took a stroll with Sugar in Green Park, crossing Horse Guards Parade to return to their apartment. Josephine was wearing her Harrods fur coat (circa 1970) not so much for warmth as for the image that it projected. A discrete blue streak set off her well coiffured hair and her lips were still 'Marilyn Monroe' scarlet. Arthur just felt that in London he should wear a suit.

On sentry duty in Whitehall, Trooper Jason Morgan sat astride a magnificent black charger named Oscar. Morgan had been in the Army for about two years and was a skilled horseman, while Oscar was an old soldier and had served more than seven years.

Like all of the horses in the Household Division, Oscar had once passed a rigorous training regime, a key part of which included not re-acting to loud noises or interference by the public. Despite this he was a difficult horse and, as the years went by, he became steadily more cantankerous.

Oscar had one notable idiosyncrasy. He would stand on three legs for long periods at a time, his front, right leg raised with the hoof about twelve inches from the ground. Sentry duty for both man and animal was boring. Oscar's eyes would glaze and sometimes one might close deceptively.

Meanwhile London's feral pigeons would scamper around the horse's feet. Oscar's seeming lack of concentration was a ruse as all the while he was waiting for a pigeon to stray into just the right position. Then without warning he would drop his right hoof and with a whoosh and a thwack he would despatch the unfortunate bird at high speed into the wall at the rear. Such was the force that the bird would be reduced to a messy heap of feathers.

Arthur and Josephine came through into Whitehall and paused to admire the sight of Trooper Morgan and Oscar, both polished and gleaming statue-like. Only a few years previously Arthur had taken a major leap into the late 20th century and bought a mobile phone. As Josephine cooed at Oscar, Arthur took a number of pictures.

Sugar was sniffing annoyingly round Oscar's hooves, but Oscar never stirred from his stance of detached boredom and Morgan maintained a steadfast gaze at an imaginary horizon. Arthur continued clicking while Josephine reached her face towards Oscar's muzzle. Suddenly, seemingly without Oscar moving a muscle, WHOOSH THWACK. The lead was snatched from Josephine's hand and Sugar was no longer there.

Morgan winced as he realised what had happened and quickly reached over and pressed the 'panic' button that sounded a bell in the Guard Room in the event of emergency. Out rushed the Corporal of Horse to be faced by a large woman in a fur coat wailing hysterically.

'Sugar, Sugar. What have you done to him?'

The Corporal of Horse looked at Morgan. 'What's happening?'

'Back wall.' said Morgan out of the side of his mouth and motioned with his head.

A quick glance revealed a tangled mass of fur against the wall. The Corporal of Horse reached over and pressed the panic button again.

'Right sir, madam, if you'll come with me, we'll see what we can sort out.'

With that he gently led Arthur and the howling Josephine into the Guard Room. Two soldiers were rushing out in response to the bell.

'Back wall.' The Corporal of Horse motioned with his head.

'Would you like to take a seat?' He waved at the tatty Guard Room easy chairs. Hot sweet tea eases most problems, he thought.

'Roberts, two teas, lad, quick.'

Trooper Roberts moved across to the table where the tea makings stood and selected the two heavy china mugs with the fewest chips and tea stains on them. He filled them and, in acknowledgement that he was in polite company, he placed them on a battered tray alongside a plastic bottle of milk and a bag of Tate and Lyle's with a sticky spoon protruding from it.

He crossed the room with the tray and jauntily announced.

'Here we are, two teas. Do you take milk and sug…'

The Corporal of Horse leaped across the room and snatched the tray from him, mercifully avoiding the chaos that such a sensitive word might provoke.

Roberts was moved by Josephine's distress and tried hard to think of some other way to help. 'Kleenex' he thought, but Guard Rooms didn't run to such luxuries. Toilet paper is the same stuff so he ran out and found, not the Andrex double quilted that graced the Beasley bathroom, but a roll of the single thickness super economy that the Army bought by the million. Nevertheless, Josephine dabbed her eyes gratefully and seemed to be gaining composure.

While all this was going on, the two soldiers had returned discretely carrying a brown cardboard box containing the remains of the late, lamented Sugar. Someone had also phoned the Regiment and asked for the Regimental Veterinary Officer to come urgently.

The Corporal of Horse struggled to think what to do next. The events would be included in the Guard Room log, but he felt it needed something more official to support the Beasley's case.

The Army has a form for everything so surely there must be something to cover it. Then it occurred to him that the Army treats a horse as a mode of transport, a vehicle, so the correct form had to be a vehicle accident form known as an FMT3.

The vet arrived and was led into a back room and shown the cardboard box. Inside was an unidentifiable bundle of fur, bedecked with several feathers from Oscar's previous victims. He returned to the Beasleys.

'I'm terribly sorry, Mr and Mrs Beasley.' he said comfortingly. 'I've examined Sugar. He must have died immediately the accident took place. There was nothing anyone could possibly have done for him.'

Josephine let out another long moan and Arthur put a comforting arm around her. When she had regained her composure Arthur continued to complete the FMT3 with the Corporal of Horse.

An FMT3 is much like the accident report forms that some insurance companies use:

Name of driver - 24067350 Trooper Morgan J

Make and type of vehicle - Horse

Name - Oscar

No - 12345

Date and time… Road conditions… Light… Weather… etc.

The final page of the form required diagrams before, on impact and after the accident. The Corporal of Horse neatly drew a horse, with rider, standing on three legs, one hoof raised with a small dog on a lead held by a lady in a fur coat. Then the horse with hoof on ground in contact with a ball of 'fur' and finally a horse with rider, standing on three legs, one hoof raised and a lady in a fur coat with hands in the air.

The Beasleys were happy to sign the form and the Corporal of Horse was keen to draw things to a conclusion.

'I think we have done all that we can today, don't you?… Are you ready to go back to your flat?… Would you like us to call you a taxi?'

'Yes, please, you've all been so kind and understanding.'

As he waved the Beasleys off, the Corporal of Horse heaved a sigh of relief at a tricky problem satisfactorily resolved. A flicker of a smile danced across his face, as he imagined the chaos and confusion that such a unique FMT3 was going to cause when it settled in the 'IN' tray of the bean counters in the Ministry of Defence whose job it was to settle such claims.

Oscar was put on 'Vet's Report', not for illness, but for temperament. He passed the bangs and noises tests again with no problems, but fortunately the vet saw fit to annotate his documents 'Not to be put on sentry duty'. Trooper Morgan secretly wished that his documents could be annotated in the same way.

In the back of the cab, Josephine dabbed her reddened eyes with her last remaining scrap of Army bog paper, while Arthur held her hand tenderly. He gazed out of the window and guiltily heaved a sigh of relief that he would no longer have to put up with that yappy, little rugrat.

11

The Snow Hole

Sleeping in a snow hole is never much fun. Contrary to expectation, it's not always cold, but it can be damp and very claustrophobic. We had navigated out to an area where the snow was very deep, dug into a bank and tunneled out a large, comfortable cave. We would use it for two nights as part of a Winter Mountain Leader Training Course held by the Scottish National Outdoor Training Centre at Glenmore Lodge in the Cairngorms.

Eric was my 'buddy'. Outside conditions were dreadful with driving snow, but we cooked our meal and settled down in our bags, as warm and comfortable as you can ever be in such circumstances.

Normal practice in a snow hole is to leave a candle burning at all times as it acts like a miner's canary and will go out if there is insufficient oxygen. Sleep is never easy and I woke several times during the night, each time feeling a little sick. At some stage the candle must have gone out, but in my dozy state I just thought it had got damp or was just 'a bloody useless candle.'

I woke early with a terrible headache and feeling of nausea. Eric felt the same as we began to prepare a breakfast of instant porridge in silence.

I struck a match and the phosphor head ignited, but straight away went out. 'Bloody useless matches have got damp.' After a dozen or so matches we managed to light my little Gaz Bluet stove, but that very quickly died. 'Bloody useless gas stove has run out, just what you want on a day like this.' Eventually we lit Eric's stove and it burned with a weak flame. I sat on the sleeping bench staring glassy-eyed. A pan of snow melted and slowly simmered while Eric sat beside me saying nothing.

Suddenly he stood up, pushed past me and forced his way through the exit. I stood to follow him and knocked the pan of near-boiling water, emptying the contents down my back. I was wearing waterproof over-trousers, the normal function of which is to keep water out. In this instance they very effectively kept the scalding water in and channeled it neatly between my buttocks.

Outside, I found Eric face down, retching in the snow. Resisting the urge to jump up and down and grab my burning backside, I rolled him over. Fortunately, the weather was calm and the cold, clean air quickly brought us both to our senses.

He was OK and we began to realise what had happened and how near we had come to disaster. The heavy snow during the night had drifted over the entry to our snow hole sealing us in. Our breathing had used up much of the oxygen and, when the candle went out, we had been too dozy to notice the significance. Our efforts to cook had used even more oxygen.

The headache and nausea are typical symptoms of carbon dioxide poisoning. Our wits were so dulled by the lack of oxygen that it was impossible to think clearly and understand what was happening. I can't say how much longer it would have been before we became unconscious, but it had been a lucky escape.

I sat Eric up in the snow. He was now looking much better.

'You OK, mate?'

'Yeah. I think so.'

'Right. Let's get inside, then. I think you need to look at me.'

I lay face down on the sleeping bench in the snow hole, baring my backside to the icy ceiling while Eric applied liberal quantities of 'Brulidine' from his first aid kit. He then found our instructor and told him what had happened and asked if we could have a bit more time to get ourselves sorted out.

He asked me if I wanted to go back to the Lodge, but I didn't feel too bad so I decided to carry on. A little later than planned, we began a long day of winter navigation practice on the snow-blasted plateau of Cairngorm. At 4pm we returned to our snow holes and prepared ourselves for our second night out.

I slept on my stomach in considerable discomfort, but was happy to take every advantage of my injured state. Each time I woke, I would nudge Eric and persuade him to get up and make sure the exit was clear of snow so that we could enjoy a much safer night.

Back at Glenmore Lodge the following evening, I unpacked my rucksack and took a shower. Immediate medical problems at the Lodge were looked after by an advanced first aider, a secondary role for one of the admin staff. It just happened that the person responsible that day was an attractive girl of about twenty-five, right in my target zone, so I was quite looking forward to going sick.

'Yes, what's the problem?' she smiled.

'I've spilt hot water down my lower back. Could you look at it for me, please?'

I lowered my trousers revealing an area of weeping flesh and blistered skin. The distinct shape of trickles of water began below my belt and disappeared between the cheeks of my backside.

'Good grief! When did you do that?'

'The day before yesterday.'

'It's terrible. You should have seen me straight away. Why on earth did you leave it so long? You should have...' She launched into a tirade of sensible medical chastisement.

'Because we were out on the hill,' was my disarming reply.

Then came the part I was looking forward to, bathing with warm water and the gentle re-application of the cream, a far nicer experience than Eric's horny, old hands.

Sadly, the pleasure was short-lived when I realised the painful depilatory effect that removing the Elastoplast that secured the huge dressing would have.

For much of the rest of the course I stood up.

12

The Letter Home

Sitting on the edge of his bed, he balanced the Basildon Bond note pad on his knee as he wrote. His bed space was in a four-man room in a portacabin in Belfast in 1972. Two months in to a four-month tour, it was just ten days to his R and R. He tried not to think about it. He didn't want to tempt fate.

Twenty-one years old, he had been in the army for almost four years, a Lance Bombardier and good at his job. His name was Mick Redman and he hailed from Plumstead. Energetic and outgoing, to his mates he was a 'chopsy Cockney', loved by all. A bright military future beckoned.

When he joined the army at seventeen, he'd left Patsy behind. They'd met at youth club and had been going steady, but neither felt inclined to get married at that age. He looked forward to seeing her each time he came home on leave and no one was surprised when two years ago, they tied the knot.

Patsy was in a married quarter back in England and wrote all the time he was away - chatty little letters about friends and family and all the little things she did. Never once did a letter reveal her true concerns. Her letters were a lifeline, a link with reality for Mick.

The Regimental Wives' Club met regularly. Patsy appreciated the support and enjoyed being part of it. They were strong women with a common bond, all worried about their menfolk.

He wrote back when time permitted, asking about home and telling stories of the successes the battery was having, always understating the danger, never down-beat, always looking forward to coming home.

The walls of the room he shared were bedecked with Playboy centrefolds and souvenirs that the lads were gathering as time went by. Centrefolds were absent from Mick's bedspace. A small Irish tricolour that he'd found when searching an empty property was the only decoration. Below, at about the height of his pillow was a picture of a smiling Patsy, propped up in bed with a new-born babe in her arms.

Beside it was a copy of the signal he had received.

> 'INFORM 25487218 L/BDR REDMAN M B CMM 17 BTY CMM THAT MRS PATRICIA REDMAN GAVE BIRTH TO A BOY 7LB 4 OZS AT AGNES BANKES HOSPITAL AT 0245 ON 4 SEP 72 STOP MOTHER AND BABY DOING WELL'

Patsy was heavily pregnant when he left. He had regular reassurances that she was well and the other wives were looking after her. Then one day the BSM met him as he came in from a patrol.

'Mick, outside, please. I need a word.'

They moved a few yards away from the portacabin. Smiling, he thrust the signal into one hand and shook the other vigorously.

'Congratulations, you've got a young son. When you're ready, we've authorised a phone call home for you. Well done young man.'

Mick struggled to hide his emotion. That evening in the Battery canteen they wet the baby's head. With a limit of two cans per day, it was hardly a rip-roaring booze up, but it was a memory that would stay with him for ever. Soon he would be with his new family.

A voice interrupted his writing.

'Ten minutes, B Section, outside in ten minutes.'

He closed his pad, dropped it in his army suitcase under the bed and prepared for the afternoon's patrol.

The patrol was led by Lieutenant Richard Balshaw. Average height, average build, from a modest family background. He had done well academically and was an outstanding sportsman, but his passion was the Army Cadet Force. Sandhurst was an obvious choice.

He had proved to be one of the best troop commanders in the regiment. His Gunnery knowledge was sound, but his greatest asset was his ability to communicate with his men and get the best out of them. Since coming to Ireland, he had been closely involved with numerous weapon finds and the arrest of several wanted men. In high pressure situations he was an example to all. He was affectionately known as 'Ballsy' as much for his approach to the job as his name.

It was a normal patrol. Eyes peeled: he was looking for the unusual. He stopped several people and checked their ID. Ops cleared them and the patrol continued. There was sporadic stone-throwing and abuse. Par for the course.

Parked cars were a concern. He was approaching a battered Ford Escort. His eye was drawn to the number plate. In the days before pressed number plates it was easy to see that the first number had been prised off, a crude method used to disguise the registration of a stolen vehicle. Dirt on the plate suggested the missing number was a four. He radioed the number and the possible alternative to Ops and moved closer.

A worried looking man walked briskly past.

The inside of the car was dirty and full of paper bags and sweet wrappers. A wire appeared to be hanging from the steering wheel. It told him what he needed to know. He was interrupted by his radio.

'… was stolen three days ago in Dunmurry. Seen in the City Centre yesterday shortly before a Post Office raid.'

'Roger, suspect the car now has a bomb in it. Request Felix and reinforcement.'

He moved away and waited for Felix, the bomb disposal officer. The rest of the battery arrived, closed the road and established a cordon round the area. Felix took a look and was in no doubt. It was obviously booby trapped. Normal form was to blow the bomb where it was.

The residents were cleared from their houses and parked cars were moved. When the area was ready Felix blew the charge. There was an almighty crump as the car exploded.

'Not much doubt about that,' said Bombardier Steve Nichol, Balshaw's second in command.

'Dead right.' He smiled in agreement.

When the dust settled Felix went forward with a forensic team to search for fragments that might give clues about the bomb. The regimental PR Officer was looking after the media, while another team moved round doing 'hearts and minds', noting damage to property and the like.

Balshaw's men were spare now so he found the incident commander and asked for permission to continue his patrol. He called Bombardier Nichol to him.

'Right, Bom we're moving off that way and back to camp. Tell the lads to stay switched on. It's not over yet.'

'Right, sir.'

Mick looked at Gunner Thomas, crouching in the next garden.

'Bloody hell, Taff, looks like Ballsy's done it again.'

They moved off with an air of confidence and turned left into the next street. Suddenly a man came down an alley alongside one of the houses, saw Mick and turned and ran. Mick dropped to one knee, rifle in the shoulder.

'Halt! Halt or I'll fire!' He ordered.

The man was taking no chances. He stopped hands in the air and turned, looking anxiously at Mick.

Mick clocked him. Late teens, six feet, slim, brown shoulder-length hair, denim jacket, dark trousers.

Bombardier Nichol had seen what happened. Balshaw arrived.

'Man behaving suspiciously, sir. Ran away when he saw Bom Redman.'

'What's your name, sir? Do you have any ID?'

Ops checked the details of his driving licence.

'Nothing on him. It all checks out.'

'Thank you, sir. Sorry to bother you.'

Still nervous, the man took his licence and scurried down the alley. Balshaw and Nichol went back to their positions and the patrol moved off.

He'd gone just a few yards when Mick's eye was caught by something in the bottom of a hedge. Half hidden, it looked like a torch.

It was a long thin flashlight, the version that took several U2 batteries, the type favoured by security men as it could double as a club. He picked it up. The dull grey body looked hardly used. Without thinking he pressed the 'ON' button.

There was a blinding white flash and in that moment his life changed for ever.

He was sitting, back against the hedge. Glassy eyes stared at the ragged sleeve where his right hand had been. An expanding red circle on his thigh indicated a shrapnel wound. His face was speckled with blood. More fragments had tattered the front of the flak jacket that had saved his life.

Nichol ripped the field dressing from Mick's webbing and somehow covered the open wound. He tied another as a tourniquet above Mick's elbow. Balshaw had already called for urgent medical evacuation.

'Christ Mick, oh Christ. It's OK, mate, OK. You'll be all right. I've got you.'

Mick stared blankly, in deep shock. He heard nothing, his ears deafened by the explosion.

***

Maureen Nichol was tidying the bedroom of her married quarter. She glanced through the widow as a car pulled up outside. Her heart raced at the sight feared by all the wives, the Families Officer and the Padre in uniform. It could only mean one thing. Something had happened in Ireland. She ran downstairs, her mind racing with thoughts of her husband, Steve.

'Oh no, not Steve, please not Steve.'

But they were walking up the path to Patsy's front door. Thoughts of Steve vanished.

'Mick, oh God, it's Mick.'

She followed in behind them and stayed with Patsy for the rest of the day. That evening Patsy and her parents landed at Aldergrove Airport in Belfast.

Mick's life was no longer in danger, but things would never be the same again.

The letter in his suitcase would remain unfinished.

13

Scruffus

Dave and Yorky laughed and joked as they confronted their mountainous 'IN' tray They were National Servicemen, a breed born to count the days, so they had no incentive to really tackle it.

Dave took the next recruit's file, Name... Rank... Trade... He noted the trade and ran his finger down a list of regiments until he found one short of soldiers in that employment. He ticked the list and typed a posting order to that regiment in the name on the file. The file with the posting order went in the 'OUT' tray.

Yorky did the same. This was the sort of boring task that could fall victim to young men with a sense of humour. Occasionally they would notice something unusual.

'Have you spotted this?' He pointed to the letters 'Scr fce' under 'Visible Distinguishing Marks'.

'What the hell does that mean?

'Dunno.'

A few files later he found another one, frowned in puzzlement and ticked the same regiment as the previous one. They laughed about it and it became fun to post the mysterious soldiers, now termed 'scruffus', all to the same regiment.

Then Dave had another idea. 'How about we post all gingers to one regiment the same way?'

All files marked 'Colour of Hair: Red' were posted to another regiment. They then added an 'under five feet four' regiment and an 'over six feet' regiment. The game had few limits as long as the correct trades were filled.

The days began to fly by and soon Yorkie was de-mobbed and returned home. Dave got on well with his replacement, but there was never the same rapport.

***

The Colonel saluted the General and invited him to inspect the parade. Generals will always stop and chat to a soldier who catches their eye. This time his eye was caught by a young man with a scar from a hair lip.

'Your trade is?'

Next, he noticed a Corporal with a scar running from the corner of his mouth.

'Where is your home?'

In the centre rank he spoke to a man with a scar across his nose from a fight, then a man scarred from ear to chin after a car accident and a man with a scar under his eye from boxing.

The CO began to see a pattern he hadn't spotted before. The RSM returned his quizzical stare and it was the subject of discussion later that day.

***

In Halifax the new clerk in the benefits office was fitting in well. He was punctual, well turned out and was learning quickly, but he was unhappy. Usually people hated National Service, but he really missed his old mate and the happy times they spent unwittingly creating a regiment with the appearance of storm troopers, each one with a 'Scar on Face' just as it had said on the files.

Civilian life had no parallel.

14

Mother's Ruin

Charlie Trebilcock was tall and broad with a weather-beaten face that told of a life in the open. 'Mother' was a perfect match: gently rounded, with rosy cheeks, a shock of curly hair and an irrepressible smile. For three generations the Trebilcocks had run Pengantle farm on an idyllic site at the end of a winding, rutted track on the rocky North Cornwall coast. It's eighty acres spanned a small zawn with a sandy beach that would make later generations of Trebilcocks wealthy. With a few cows, pigs and chickens and a huge garden they were almost self-sufficient.

Dennis Trebilcock was nine when the war ended and although he was well aware of it, he hadn't been greatly affected. His father, Charlie, had a 'wheezy' chest and this, along with his important role as a farmer, meant that he was not called to serve in uniform.

He left school at fifteen and settled in to the farm routine. Each morning, in all weathers, he and Charlie would rise at five to feed the animals. Back in at seven thirty, they would warm themselves by the Aga as Mother made a huge breakfast. Then they washed and shaved at a mirror hung above the kitchen sink. The rest of the day's work was preceded by a call for the 'morning constitutional' at the dilapidated shed way down at the end of the garden, that housed the bucket toilet.

'Morning, Mr Pascoe.' Dennis greeted the old postman as he walked up the garden path.

'Morning, Dennis, Summink for you today.' He handed him a brown envelope.

Mother looked over his shoulder as he sat at the kitchen table and opened it. It was his call-up papers for National Service. A few weeks later, with Mother and Dennis in the front and the younger brothers bumping around in the back, Charlie drove the Land Rover to St Erth station where they waved a sad farewell to the eldest son.

Dennis was met by a recruiting Sergeant and taken to the Depot where he would start his basic training. It was hard, but he was fit from life on the farm and he took to it like a duck to water. After all, reveille at six thirty was a 'lie-in' for him.

A letter on YMCA paper would drop on the mat each Monday morning and Mother would quietly read of his many adventures. Weeks later the family again climbed in to the rickety Rover and drove, this time, to Bodmin where they watched with pride as Dennis marched past on completion of his basic training. Mother dabbed a tear.

Life with the battalion in Catterick was interesting and exciting. Dennis loved the camaraderie and, away from home, he grew up.

The week's training was on explosive devices. On the first afternoon an accident occurred on the range and a soldier was hit by shards of metal. The injury was not life-threatening, but needed urgent medical attention, so Dennis drove the Platoon Sergeant and the patient to hospital.

It was almost midnight when they got back to camp, so the duty cook rustled up egg banjos for all and Dennis slouched to his barrack room. He was excused parade the next morning, so dropped everything and, exhausted, just crashed out.

Next day he polished his boots and tidied his kit neatly into his locker. When he picked up his webbing he remembered that in his ammunition pouch was a tobacco tin with a small piece of plastic explosive and a fuse kit that he was ready to set up before the accident. The Army is very strict about the control of ammunition and explosives. It should have been handed in before he left the range, but in his hurried departure it had been missed. It was only a small quantity so 'what the hell'. He threw it in the back of his locker and thought nothing more of it.

Dennis's life as a National Serviceman was full and active. He worked hard and played hard, but as his time drew to a close he looked forward to returning to the quiet beauty of Pengantle and the warmth of his family home.

He rose with his father at five thirty, fed the animals, shaved in the kitchen and slipped effortlessly back into the old routine, but something was lacking. He missed the buzz and immediacy of army life and had grown used to its twentieth century comforts.

By comparison, his family and the farm were stuck in a bygone age and he couldn't drag them out of it. Main drains were yet to come to the area. The primitive bucket toilet at the end of the garden burned his mind and epitomised all that annoyed him about his old home.

Filled with anger and despair, he sat on the cliff top and gazed thoughtfully across the sea towards America. He stood up and strode purposefully back to the house.

When he left the battalion, the Quartermaster had allowed him to keep a number of issued items that the army didn't want back. He opened the drawer: his boot brushes, his housewife, army socks and clasp knife. Memories came flooding back. His eye was taken by the battered tobacco tin with the explosives still in it. He picked it up and knew what he must do.

Eyes fixed on the privy, he strode down the garden path, opened the tin and carefully placed the explosives under the old shed.

'Watya doin', son?' His father confronted him.

'That's it, dad I'm up to here with this place. That privy is the most disgustin' thing I know. It's gotta go. I'm gonna blow it up.'

'No son, don't do that.'

'I've made up my mind, dad. It's too late.'

'No, son, Mother's in that privy.'

At that moment a deafening explosion filled the air with fragments of scorched timber. As the smoke cleared they were faced with a scene of complete destruction. At the centre of a charred circle Mother still sat on the bench seat over the bucket.

'Mother, oh, mother. I'm so sorry. Are you OK?'

Her clothes were tattered. Her face was blackened and her lovely curls were now Brillo. Her red-rimmed eyes were wide with confusion. She croaked.

'Yes son, I'm all right. It must have been something I ate.'

That, sir, is a shaggy dog story

15

The King of Tonga

In the late Sixties, there were two types of overseas cadets at Sandhurst, those who came near the top of their nations' military academies and those who were there for diplomatic reasons. The Crown Prince of Tonga fell firmly into the latter category.

He established his reputation right from day one when Company Sergeant Major Dan Fogarty, a broad Cockney was calling the roll for the new intake.

'Brown… Jones… Smith… Prince Tapi… Tuppow… Blimey, sir, how the hell do you pronounce this?'

'Actually it's Tupouto'a, sir, but you can call me George!'

So it was that Prince Tupouto'a of Tonga was known as 'George' by everyone from Commandant to cleaner throughout his time at Sandhurst.

George was the grandson of Queen Salote of Tonga, who captured the hearts of the British people by insisting, despite the heavy rain, on riding in an open carriage at the Queen's Coronation.

He was charming and urbane and won everyone over with his cultured diction and perfect English manners. At Sandhurst he was treated like every other officer cadet. He played his part to the full and took the knocks with all the others.

Like many of the 'diplomatic' entries, he struggled with the physical aspects of the course, but his colleagues were never going to see him fail and always saw him through. He in turn treated then as equals and most week-ends would go with a group to London. The Tongan royal family had a flat in Westminster and George would have his friends overnight, sleeping on the floor and settees.

On one occasion, the King and Queen arrived for a month's stay. Unfortunately, George had failed to note this in his diary so, when the King opened the door to his London flat after a tiring long-haul flight he was faced with a dishevelled group of stinking, hung-over officer cadets waking from a night of drunken revelry. The King was every bit as laid back as George and took it all in his stride, delighted to see his son again.

When the King and Queen were not in the flat, George continued to use it. His friends met them on several times, when they were always as charming and friendly as their son.

Back at Sandhurst conversations about George's parents always referred to them as 'Mr and Mrs King'!

There is an excellent tale about how Mr King, otherwise known as King Tupou IV, was attending an official reception in the UK and was bored with two other guests arguing about which one had the most aristocratic Scottish ancestry. The King quietly remarked.

'I, too, have some Scottish blood in me… '

Then, deadpan, he continued. 'Grandfather ate a Scottish missionary.'

Stories from George's life in the tropical paradise would always amuse. In the second term, the syllabus focussed on swimming and everyone had to pass a very challenging test. George was placed in the group of weaker swimmers and was splashing around one day when the exasperated PT Instructor remarked.

'Blimey, sir, how is it you come from a sunshine island and can't blooming swim?'

'Well actually, Staff, when I was a boy my nurse used to take me down to the lagoon. I would float on my back and she would just pull me around.'

The Sovereign's parade in December 1968, when George passed out, was one of the few occasions when he received special attention as among the proud parents spectating were 'Mr and Mrs King'. The occasion can be viewed on YouTube.

George's father had ruled as an absolute monarch and, on his death in 2006, there was considerable civil unrest. George was sensitive to this and delayed his coronation saying that he would work to bring democracy. In the next two years he put together a framework for political reform and three days before his coronation in 2008 he ceded most of his executive powers to a democratically-elected parliament.

It was forty years since George had left Sandhurst, but he had retained contact with four particular friends (two British, an Iranian and a Kiwi) and invited them to Tonga for the festivities. Bill Lamin, then a Cornish school teacher was George's roommate during their 'traumatic' first term and he wrote a highly amusing account of how the four of them had rubbed shoulders with international statesmen in five days of unusual Tongan feasting and celebration.

King George Tupou V of Tonga proved a very popular monarch much loved by his people. He was famed for his eccentricities, like travelling around the island in a black London cab because it was 'the most sensible form of transport when wearing spurs and a sword'. He regularly wore a monocle and top hat (or when wearing uniform a white pith helmet) and always carried a cane. He also liked to play with model boats in the palace swimming pool.

George died in 2008 at the age of only sixty-four and was succeeded by his brother, Tupou VI.

You wonder how a person like George with such a revered and protected upbringing could have ever had true friends. Perhaps it's a sign of the quality of the training at Sandhurst with its shared hardships that the bonds forged at that time had lasted so long. It is also a sign of the wonderful loyalty of the man that after so many years he never forgot those old friends, despite his exalted status.

16

The Mountaineering Instructors Certificate

The Mountaineering Instructors Certificate is a high-level civilian qualification enabling you to teach mountaineering and lead expeditions at any time of year in the UK. In 1975 I undertook a rigorous assessment over a period of five days at the National Mountaineering Centre, Plas-Y-Brenin.

One of the tests I was most wary of was the 'mountain day', when each student walked for a day with an assessor whose aim was to chat and discover the candidate's attitude to the hills and his mountain ethos. The civilian mountain training establishment was then, and probably it still is, very left wing. They believed that the hills were for recreation and learning and harboured a deep suspicion of the services who wanted to use the mountains more rigorously as a testing environment to promote military leadership.

It was a one-to-one assessment and testing me was a woman who was a well-known senior lecturer at a teacher training college. The omens were not good.

We took out our maps at the start in Llanberis Pass.

'Right, we're here. I want you to take me up the flank to the Horseshoe and on to Snowdon summit. Then down to the Miners' Track and finish at Pen-y-Pass. OK?'

The day was clear and I was familiar with the route. I took a precautionary bearing, did some calculations and we set off. We chatted at a leisurely pace and I was asked the simple question.

'Would you take a group of eleven-year-olds up Snowdon today?'

'Yes, I think so.'

'Isn't it a bit breezy?'

Not content with a simple answer, I dug myself a hole.

'It may be, but get 'em out and give them a bit of excitement. There's nothing worse than seeing a group of kids trek up the Miners' Track, sit down on the rocks and their teacher say to them, 'Look, there's Snowdon – up there.' Give them an adventure.'

She pushed me into my hole.

'And don't you think for deprived children who have never been out of the inner city that it's an adventure in itself just to come to the mountains of Wales?'

'Well, I suppose so.'

'And what do you mean by adventure?'

This was a question I could cope with, but, with shovel still in hand, I promptly dug myself deeper.

'An adventure should have challenge, excitement, risk… It requires courage and determination and should end with a sense of achievement…'

These were the things we sought to promote on the military courses that we ran, exactly the 'gung-ho' stuff that ran contrary to the civilian perception of the use of the mountains. In one move I had reinforced her perceived prejudices of the military. My heart sank as I realised my error.

We strolled on in silence.

‘Where are we now?’ she asked casually.

‘About here.’ I replied, putting a fat finger on the map.

‘No, where are we *exactly*?’

I was momentarily thrown. It was a clear day and we could see where we were going, so I had not been concentrating on detailed navigation. After all, this was the ‘mountain day’, the navigation test was yet to come. I orientated the map.

‘Well, that feature is that one there and that… so I reckon we are here.’ I pointed accurately on the map with a pen.

‘You should always know where you are in the mountains to the nearest ten metres. What would have happened if there had been an accident?’

With hindsight, she probably couldn’t have known more accurately where we were herself, but she sure knew how to pile on the pressure. We strode on and eventually reached the summit of Snowdon.

‘Right, let’s have lunch.’

I was dejected and felt sure I had blown my chances, but I reasoned that things could not get any worse. I threw down my rucksack and took out my lunch box, eagerly anticipating the cheering sugar hit that I might get from a thickly spread, strawberry jam sandwich. I had abandoned the shovel long ago, but my guard was down.

‘How would you describe the difference between a teacher, a leader, a coach and a trainer?’

I blinked in disbelief. She was now feeding *my* prejudices of the civilian mountain training profession. This was just the sort of semantic garbage I imagined teacher-trainers discussed as they sat cross-legged on the floor joyfully devouring lentils and yoghurt.

I gave the question careful consideration, sandwich poised in mid-air, and, in that moment, one of Snowdon's many seagulls swooped down and stole it clean from my grasp. It flew off, thus depriving me of my longed-for carbohydrate boost.

I was wrong, things could get worse and it *was* all downhill from there; downhill to the Miners' Track and downhill with my spirits.

That evening the Warden of Plas-Y-Brenin called me into his office. Strangely there was no mention of my attitude to the hills, but he told me that my navigation had not been up to standard. I would be rigorously tested on 'navigation day'. This was just the confidence boost I needed that evening, as I went in to sit a long, written paper on mountain weather.

There were four in our group for the navigation day and I was given the first leg – pressure on right from the start. The assessor was a person I knew quite well, but there was no chance of favours. I was feeling good and dug my heel in with confidence when we reached the first objective. I was similarly confident with the two legs that I had to navigate later on and, unlike the previous day, things went well.

I passed the navigation assessment and was relieved to learn that my overall performance was good enough to be awarded the MIC. It was a valuable and highly respected qualification which few servicemen held at that time.

In years to come, it was to stand me in good stead when applying for jobs in the service mountain training world, even if my meat-polluted military brain never appreciated the difference between a teacher, a leader, a coach and a trainer.

17

Hydrotherapy

My clothes were stuffed in my sports bag and jammed in the locker. I breathed deeply and inhaled the unpleasant smell of chlorine. Was I beach-body ready? Should I have sharpened my educated doggy-paddle? Too late, brace up and stride manfully to the pool.

Jane greeted me. A group were already in the water. In a variety of shapes and sizes, most, like me, were pensioners. One thing was certain, Speedos were out, so I had nothing to worry about.

For years I had struggled with arthritis in many of my joints. A knee replacement had left me with stiffness and pain that neither the clinical staff nor the physiotherapists could do any more to improve. A friend asked if I'd tried hydrotherapy.

Trim and extrovert, Jane was what I was looking for as a remedial trainer. She assessed my physical abilities and I agreed to go give hydrotherapy a try.

She was running warm-up exercises from the side of the pool and about eighteen people were following her moves in the water, so I joined in. When she finished, the group spread out to begin their own exercise programmes and Jane called me over. She gave me a laminated sheet of exercises that she had devised for me and briefly took me through each one.

Then, on my own, I began my first exercise. Beside me a woman's head bobbed above a round dark mass. About five-foot two, she was doing step-ups. When she stood fully upright it was apparent that she possessed the most magnificent treasure chest. She placed her thumbs under the straps of her black swimsuit and gave a mighty heave upwards. I wondered what purpose it served and averted my gaze.

I edged closer to the man next to me. We nodded. His hair was dyed chestnut and neatly parted Sixties-style. His non-beach-ready-body was tanned nut brown. Neon green swim shorts completed the image of 'Sandbanks Man'. I bet he drives a four by four. I took a liking to him.

I looked around at the rest of the group. Only about four were men. It was interesting to note how the two sexes approached the session differently. The men focussed on each task conscientiously and moved from exercise to exercise talking to no one. Later, they bonded in the changing room with manly chat about soccer and the other important things in life. By contrast, for the women, it was much more of a social event and they would regularly pause and chat. Pat and Linda, in their black swimsuits, spent most of the time in animated conversation in the corner by the steps, only occasionally waving a leg left or right under the water.

As people finished their exercise programmes they began to leave the pool. This was a moment of realisation. In the pool we moved with ease, now several gripped the handrail tightly as they climbed the steps and limped to their sticks and crutches. Smiling, they hobbled to the changing room leaving me humbled by my comparatively good mobility.

On the second week I entered the pool with confidence. Jane waved, Sandbanks Man nodded, this time in electric pink swim shorts. The magnificent treasure chest smiled and

I averted my gaze. I began the warm-up with enthusiasm focusing on Jane, closely following her moves.

Then it happened. Stretching left, my hand touched the strap of a black swimsuit. It was a mere brush, but an electric shock shot up my arm and I recoiled. We looked at each other in acute embarrassment, moved two steps apart and carried on self-consciously.

I began my own exercise programme. Next to me was a lady, a pensioner with jet black hair neatly tied back. Gold drop earrings, a heavy gold necklace and gold bangles bedecked her generous, teak-tanned body, Gold braid decorated the straps of her black swimsuit – super bling! It was Sandbanks Lady. I looked to see if the gold was real or if the imitation was leaving tell-tale green marks on her skin.

The magnificent treasure chest was exercising next to a lady in a black swimsuit with bingo wings. Treasure chest or bingo wings? I wondered which made the best flotation aid. But then, they were probably wondering if my man-boobs achieved the same thing.

A severely disabled teenager arrived in a wheel chair. A gantry with a chair hanging from it was slotted into a socket on the side of the pool. A team lifted the boy on to the chair and lowered him in. He was received in the water and almost immediately splashed around unaided, laughing happily at the freedom that the water gave him.

Meanwhile Pat and Linda chatted in the corner by the steps.

After eight weeks Jane gave me a review. Supported by the water, I was able to exercise much harder than on the land and we were both pleased with my progress. I asked if she would step up my programme and she suggested that I continued with what I was doing but used weights. The ‘weights’ were actually polystyrene blocks that strapped round the ankle and provided resistance when the foot was moved.

They were working well and my next exercise was a simple breast stroke leg kick while floating on my back. Without thinking, I lay back expecting to float, but my ‘weighted’ polystyrene ankles popped quickly and uncontrollably to the surface. At the same time and at roughly the same speed, my head dipped down towards the floor of the pool. I splashed wildly in rising panic, trying desperately to keep my head above water.

A vacant youth, in yellow shirt and red shorts was seated on a tennis umpire’s chair. Denied his digital device, he stared open-mouthed at a non-existent horizon. All round me pensioners looked on, not knowing what to do.

‘Oh dear, that man’s drowning in the shallow end. I can’t save him as I’ll have to touch his naked body and I’m only wearing my black swimsuit.’

Pat and Linda paused their conversation in the corner by the steps and gazed anxiously.

Then a stroke of luck, in my wild thrashings my hand touched a lady nearby. I gripped her shoulder like a Scotsman with a five-pond note. My other hand clasped her behind the neck in a tight embrace and, mercifully, a foot touched the floor. I gasped with relief, my head resting on her shoulder in an over-familiar manner. Panting uncontrollably, I dribbled chlorinated water down the front of her black swimsuit. We quickly separated, I thanked her profusely and spluttered an apology for the embarrassment I had caused.

The youth in red and yellow stifled a yawn and was now standing, watching as I threw my weights at the wall and waded to the steps.

Sandbanks man came over and asked if I was OK. At last we had time for a proper conversation. It transpired he was a retired builder, named Eric, from Kinson. He probably drove a Ford. Kind of destroyed the pigeon hole that I'd put him in.

A fit-looking seventy-year-old cruised past us in her black swimsuit with an effortless crawl… one, two, breathe… one, two, breathe.,, She narrowly missed Pat and Linda who were chatting in the corner by the steps.

Drama over, life in the pool was back to normal.

And so it has continued each Monday for almost eight years. Hydrotherapy has helped offset the frustration of my limitations in the gym and has eased me back into creaking action after several more minor ops. More than anything, I enjoy it.

Christmas is coming…

Must buy my wife a black swimsuit.

18

P Company

P Company is the physical selection course that all ranks must pass before they go for parachute training. It is recognised as one of the most physically demanding courses in the services. In my day, before joining 148 Battery all members had to complete it. I did so in Aldershot in 1974.

The course was four weeks long with a period of 'beasting' in preparation for the tests that Airborne Forces demanded to prove a candidate's worthiness to serve with them. There were no frills or padding, each day consisted of a heavy period of physical activity in the morning and a second in the afternoon, interspersed with relatively unimportant films or lectures during which we fought to stay awake.

Normal military activities were given a special P Company twist. Even though I was never a strong swimmer I could just about pass the Army Swimming Test. 'Swimming' on the programme looked to be a welcome break from constantly running in boots and denims, but oh no, not the P Company way. The first thing was a dive, not a jump, off the three-metre board. As I and many others tried to conceal our apprehension a couple of smug looking individuals piped up.

'Staff, we're non-swimmers.'

'That's OK, lads. Someone will fish you out.'

So the non-swimmers sort of fell off the three-metre board, came up spluttering and were fished out by the life-saver, to the cheers and admiration of the rest of us.

So it continued, with each activity becoming more outrageous until the grand finale. Aldershot Military Swimming Pool had a second diving platform at the shallow end and, what we hadn't noticed, a trapeze bar suspended from the roof above the middle of the pool.

First exercise: you are handed the bar standing on the platform at the shallow end and you swing across on the trapeze to the platform at the deep end. Some achieved it. OK so far.

Second exercise: the bar is swung to you as you stand on the platform at the shallow end. You jump and catch the moving bar and swing over to the other platform. Most people crash in and apprehension starts to mount.

Third exercise: you catch the bar and as you swing over you release the bar at the mid-point and enter the water in an elegant Tom Daley, tariff 9.5 dive. This was impossible for anyone to get right. We all cheered and roared at the crashing, stinging entries that we made. Constipation was never a problem on P Company.

Conventional activities in the gym were also given the P Company treatment. I could get away with all the usual vaults at school, but P Company's vaulting was conducted like a parachuting exercise. In the aircraft the first man stands in the door with the remainder up tight behind him. When the green light comes on the dispatcher screams 'GO… GO… GO…' and taps each man on the shoulder in quick succession as the signal to jump.

The vaulting box was set up at the end of the gym on all five sections, with a beat board for take-off. Two PTIs stood-in at the box for safety and another acted like the dispatcher, screaming. 'GO… GO… GO…' to set us on our way. The aim was to have two people running up as the first person was clearing the box. We would keep going, vaulting time and again, getting ever more tired and breathless until we were told to stop or, more likely, there was a hilarious heap (P Company humour).

Panting like an old man, I misjudged the take-off, clipped the box and brought the top section down on top of me as I lay on my back on the safety mat. Seemingly oblivious, the dispatcher kept up his 'GO… GO… GO…' and numbers two, three, four, five and others behind them soared over the box into what became the gym version of a motorway pile up.

With bodies lying everywhere, amid peals of laughter one of the PTIs, an Army Judo champion, came to see how I was.

'You OK, sir.'

'Yes, staff.' I attempted a smile, pushed the top section of the box off my chest and tried to get to my feet.

'Well done, sir. I thought you threw that box superbly!'

On other occasions a 45-minute gym period would consist of an indoor assault course made up from the various pieces of gym apparatus. All quite straight forward, except that we would go round again and again and again, never told what would be the last lap, until we were absolutely shattered. Then we would play a game called 'It pays to be a winner' where we would race round the course and the first one in would go to the changing room and so on until we were down to the last five. These were quite obviously ‘the wasters’ and were sent in together in complete ignominy.

Probably the thing people most remember about P Company is milling. Each of us was paired off with another of similar weight and build, and given sixty seconds to demonstrate 'controlled physical aggression' in a milling contest. A ring was formed from gym benches and fighters wore 6oz boxing gloves.

Milling is similar to boxing except neither winning, losing, nor skill are pre-requisites. Instead, candidates are scored on their courage, determination and aggression. Blocking, ducking and weaving result in points deducted.

Most people found themselves paired against a person of similar weight, but at the top end of the scale weights varied significantly. Staff Sergeant MacQueenie looked at me.

‘Looks like you’ve got Gascoigne, sir. Bit heavier than you, but you won’t mind that will you?’

At 12st 4lbs I was the fourth heaviest on the course, Gascoigne was the next, almost a stone heavier and taller. I adopted what I thought was an air of nonchalance and nodded. My father had been a great fight fan and I boxed at school, but I never kept it up. I felt I wasn’t particularly good.

Junior Lance Bombardier ‘Bamber’ Gascoigne was from the Junior Leaders Regiment RA, one of a number of units that in those days took lads straight from school at 15 ½ and trained them as soldiers. At 17½ they would ’muster’ and be sent to join regular army units.

‘Bamber’ Gascoigne was hoping to join 7 Parachute Regiment Royal Horse Artillery (7 RHA). At seventeen he was quiet and cautious, despite being big, strong, very fit and one of the stars of the course. MacQueenie was from 7 RHA so he took a particular interest in Gascoigne and the other Gunners going through P Company, as he might subsequently find himself serving with them.

I was obviously in for a hard time and MacQueenie was going to make the most of it. Gascoigne looked surprisingly nervous in his corner, but MacQueenie put his face by his ear and growled.

'Right, lad, now's your big chance and all the boys are all relying on you. See that over there eh? That's an officer, that is. Look at 'im eh? Wha' d'ya think? This is gonna be the one time in all your Army life that you'll get a chance to snot an officer, eh? So don't waste it. Get out there and give it some wellie and make sure you don't let the lads down.'

In the other corner I struggled to maintain my nonchalant air as my legs had turned to jelly. I remembered the advice my father had once given me.

'If you're ever faced by a bigger opponent or insurmountable odds, make sure you land the first punch. Then, if you subsequently get pasted, you should have the satisfaction of having done *some* damage.'

The bell sounded and, with my father's words in mind, I took two strides across the ring and swung a mighty right-hander. It caught the unsuspecting Bamber smack on the nose before he had a chance to get his gloves up. What happened afterwards was like something from the Incredible Hulk as Bamber was transformed into a raging monster.

Arms rained hammer blows from all directions. For what seem like the longest sixty seconds in my life I could do little more than keep swinging my arms pointlessly and picking myself up off the floor. Bamber Gascoigne didn't let the lads down, but, as my father predicted, I had the minor satisfaction of landing one terrific blow.

Bamber spent 22 years in 7 RHA rising to the rank of Staff Sergeant and was one of the most popular characters in the Regiment. I met him and MacQueenie on a number of occasions over the years, usually with a glass in hand. Great friendships are forged in adversity!

Milling still features in today's P Company, but fighters now wear head guards and gum shields – say no more.

On P Company Officers and Senior NCOs were expected to set the example. They always ran at the back of the squad, the most difficult place to run, and were expected to help and encourage the weaker members if they flagged. The staff showed no sympathy or compassion. When a man dropped back and lost contact with the squad, that was it. He was unceremoniously bundled into the follow-up Land Rover and his course was usually over.

The high-level confidence area was another important test. It consisted of swings and rope traverses more than twenty feet above the ground with no safety nets. Our tests were done on a wet day and several were wheeled off in the 'meat waggon' when they lost their grip and fell.

The most daunting obstacle was the 'Trainasium', a scaffold tower more than forty feet high, much higher than a house. You climb up the side to the start of a pathway of scaffold boards which you run along. There are gaps several feet wide between successive boards which you jump. One board is on a seesaw while on others the landing board is much lower than the take-off, so the gap looks wider and even more daunting. At the top is a pair of bars, about shoulder width apart and about ten feet long. You stand tall and proud on these and shuffle along to halfway where you halt and call out your name, rank and number. Two shackles are bolted here so you have to physically lift each foot and step over them to continue. A refusal at any point is an automatic 'fail' for the whole course.

The final week consisted of fearsome endurance tests in the mountains of Brecon.

On the final day the course assembled in a hangar. About sixty started only about twenty finished. I sat next to Richard Bethell, a Scots Guards officer who had become a particular friend.

'How do you think you've done?' He asked.

'I don't really know. I hope I've done enough. I don't think I could have done better, but I'll tell you what. I'd never want to put myself through all that again.'

'Me neither.'

The results were declared with typical P Company directness. The Company Commander called your name, you stood up and he simply said 'Pass' or 'Fail'.

'Jones.'

'Sir.'

'Fail.'

'Boldngrey.'

'Sir.'

'Pass.' Whoopee! I couldn't believe it. I was relieved and delighted beyond measure.

Now all I had to do now was jump out of an aircraft, easy enough. Or was it? Parachute accidents only happen to one in how many millions?

With my relationship with Murphy and his 'law' I wondered if there might be problems!

19

The Wisdom of Alan

One of the great things about military life is the lasting friendships that you make. They are usually formed in adversity and based on mutual understanding which has few parallels in civilian life. Alan is one such friend. We occupied next door rooms when we began our military careers at Sandhurst fifty-eight years ago and have remained friends ever since.

His career was fairly short, but in that time he led a remarkable and varied life and despite his youth and inexperience was given huge responsibility.

From Sandhurst Alan served in a regiment in Germany, initially with a gun battery and later as the Assistant Adjutant. The Adjutant is effectively the Chief Executive Officer of the regiment.

Alan's CO was a fiery character who sacked the Adjutant a few months after Alan's appointment. The same fate befell the next two incumbents. In six months there were three Adjutants and the postings branch couldn't find another replacement at short notice. Alan stood in on each occasion so became the Adjutant of an 800-man regiment at the age of twenty-two, a post normally filled by someone around thirty.

He then volunteered to serve on secondment to the Sultan of Oman's Armed Forces (SAF). After three months of an intensive Arabic language course and numerous lectures and briefings he flew out for what he described as 'The start of the most extraordinary adventure, part Boys Own, part North West Frontier.'

When the aircraft landed in Muscat, in northern Oman in forty degrees of heat he experienced for the first time the unforgettable smell of the desert 'an exotic, heady mix of hot sand, spices and goat dung'. After five days of briefings and administration he was flown 500 miles south to the province of Dhofar. In Dhofar the Sultan's Armed Forces were fighting a war against Communist insurgents infiltrating from the Yemen.

Alan was heavily involved in artillery actions from the start. It is worth noting that between the end of the Aden campaign in 1967 and the Falklands War in 1982 the Royal Artillery did not fire a shot in anger, so his experience was unusual.

After five months he was due a period in the peaceful north, away from the fighting. His CO called him in for a progress report and what he expected to be a pat on the back.

At that time the Sultan's Armed Forces were expanding rapidly to meet the Communist threat and the single battery of Oman Artillery was being increased to a regiment. To his great surprise, still officially a Lieutenant in the British Army, Alan was promoted Major and, for the rest of his time in Oman, commanded a battery.

Alan's battery was initially based in Muscat in a barracks tucked under Jebel Akhdar near the little town of Rostaq. As the senior military commander his position in the local community required him to pay a formal visit to the Wali, or headman, of the Rostaq district. It was customary to demonstrate status by arriving with a large entourage, so a couple of three-ton trucks were loaded with soldiers, all armed and in their smartest uniforms.

The Wali occupied Rostaq Fort, which has dominated the area for hundreds of years. Askars, the Wali's private bodyguard, guarded the gates, armed with old Martini Henry rifles, often decorated with silver.

The party was led to the Diwan (the council chamber) where the Wali was holding court with the Qadi, (the judge) and the elders. They were all seated on cushions around the walls. Alan was met with great courtesy, and after much handshaking and exchanging formal greetings they were invited to sit with the Wali as he continued to listen to the locals who were petitioning him.

After a while retainers served halwa, the traditional Arabic sweetmeat containing nuts and cardamom seeds, followed by qahwa, Arabic coffee, poured from a brass coffee pot into thimble shaped porcelain cups. Alan occasionally looked to one of his Omani officers to help translate and make sure that he observed the correct protocols.

A few days later the Wali, with an entourage of about thirty askars, swept into Oman Artillery's camp in a convoy of Land Rovers and Alan and his team returned the compliment in a more European manner.

A good personal relationship with the Wali and Qadi paid off some months later when he was unwittingly drawn into a civil legal matter.

He writes:

'I received a message that one of my soldiers was in the Wali's jail, a medieval dungeon in the fort. As the soldier was subject to military discipline the Wali would be happy to release him into my custody, provided I would hear the case against him. It turned

out that this soldier was due to get married in a match arranged between his and the bride's parents.

He had other ideas, though, and wanted to marry another girl from his village whom he had known since childhood. Instead of following the correct procedure, he had taken matters into his own hands, eloped with the girl, and then given himself up to the Wali of Rostaq.'

The three fathers and various other relatives crowded into Alan's little office and sat on cushions round the walls. After half an hour of coffee and pleasantries, they got down to business.

He writes:

'My Arabic was getting better, but it didn't stretch to understanding the intricacies of Omani marriage rights, so (an Omani officer) acted as my translator'.

The soldier had insulted the families of the two girls and brought shame on his own family. Dealing with him was relatively easy. Alan sentenced him to fourteen days detention in the cells of the Guard Room of Oman Artillery.

Dealing with the families was much more difficult.

He writes:

'It took a couple of hours, but eventually they agreed a suitable pay off in goats to the father of the espoused and now rejected girl and a similar bride price for the girl who had eloped and wanted to marry her beau.'

With more hand shaking the various parties departed, satisfied with the result, while Alan withdrew to the Mess for a stiff drink!

After ten months in the calm of Muscat He took his battery back to Dhofar and spent the following ten months on active service. Oman Artillery continued its expansion and, at one stage, he was commanding thirteen guns and four heavy mortars!

On one operation he and his radio operator, Fazal, were attached to an Iranian Brigade that was supporting the Sultan's Armed Forces.

He writes:

Food on the jebel was a perennial problem. We scrounged 'compo' rations from the British units in Salalah, and occasionally bought whatever tinned food was on sale at the cold store in the town, or else survived on the SAF operational rations. Fazal and I ran low on food. I was down to my last tin of compo; He had some khubz (bread). The problem was that my tin was of pork luncheon meat, and clearly 'haram', forbidden for a Muslim.'

This might appear a simple problem, but it posed an interesting moral dilemma. If Alan told Fazal that it was pork, he would have to refuse and go hungry. To offer it to him and deny that it was pork might to a European seem a white lie. However deceiving a Moslem into eating pork is a serious matter. But, if Alan said nothing and Fazal didn't ask, he could claim ignorance and eat it unknowingly. If he later realised that it was pork he could pray for forgiveness.

After two wonderful years, Alan sadly left Oman. Back home he reverted to the rank of Lieutenant and was promoted Acting Captain, but he would never forget that 'heady mix of hot sand, spices and goat dung'.

His next job was as an instructor teaching Officer Cadets at Sandhurst, a far cry from the responsibility and excitement of commanding thirteen guns and four mortars in battle as he had done in the months before his twenty-fifth birthday. It's very unlikely that he would have achieved responsibility like that in the British Army until he was about forty. Few Europeans will have experienced the Arab culture involved with a marriage dispute and used goats for compensation!

He left the Army shortly after and, not surprisingly, enjoyed a very successful civilian career. In retirement he devotes much of his time to voluntary work and plays a prominent role in his village's Remembrance Ceremony.

Only the observant would notice that one unusual medal that he proudly wears is a Sultan's award for gallantry.

20

The Grepon

I stepped off the train and smelled the crisp mountain air, Chamonix the Mecca for Alpine climbers since the days of the pioneers of mountaineering. Welcoming blue skies, shining snow and hard, warm, friendly granite, it was my favourite playground.

I heaved my rucksack on to my back and headed for the campsite where Pete and Babs were waiting. They had travelled in their camper van with Gary, their two-year-old son. Babs put the kettle on while Gary played happily on the grass and Pete and I caught up with our news. We had been instructors together at the Joint Services Mountain Training Centre in Wales and we wanted to pack as much climbing into our ten-day holiday as possible.

That afternoon we strolled into town for vital supplies, red wine, baguettes and cheese. Next, we renewed our acquaintance with Maurice, 'le patron' of the Bar Nat, the favourite pub of impoverished Brits. Then off to drool, once again, at the shiny equipment in Snell Sport, a treasure house for mountaineers. Most importantly, we visited the Bureau des Guides and checked the 'meteo' for the next few days.

That evening we decided that our first route should be the Mer de Glace face of the Grépon (4,382 metres). The Chamonix Alps are famous for their pinnacle ridges, with features like the Grepon known as 'aiguilles'.

The East Face of Grépon was first climbed in 1911 by the Swiss guide Josef Knubel with, the British Alpine pioneers,

O G Jones and G W Young. At the time it was one of the most difficult routes in the Alpes. The Grepon sits on a spur overlooking the beautiful glacier known as the Mer de Glace. The route is about 850m long with a guide book time of eight hours. It promised spectacular views of the Mont Blanc massif and appeared to be within our technical ability.

The weather forecast was good, so at about 2pm we set off on the picturesque Montenvers cog railway to the little station perched above the Mer de Glace. From there we followed a winding footpath that rose up the side wall of the glacier to the Bivouac de la Tour-Rouge. The Alps are dotted with a network of bivouacs, or mountain huts, that provide shelter for climbers as they travel through the area. These huts vary in sophistication from comfortable mountain hotels to garden sheds, perched on precipices.

The Tour Rouge came in the latter category. At the time of writing, the guide book describes it as a ruin and unusable. When we used it, wooden boards were missing from the walls, but it provided a dry shelter from which we could begin our route the following day. Most importantly, it cost nothing.

We set off at dawn and crunched across the snow to the start of the rock. Chamonix granite is warm, rough and friendly and the early stages of our route were quite straightforward. At one point the guide book told us to abseil down into a gully and climb the wall on the other side. We did so without noticing that we would not be able to climb back up the rock that we had abseiled down, so effectively, from that point on we had no retreat.

It was a superb day and the views were as spectacular as the guide book had promised, but following the route was difficult and we were breathing hard because of the altitude.

As the day wore on the aiguille seemed to be getting no closer and we began to worry that we would be beaten by darkness.

At about 8pm we decided we would have to spend the night out so we found a flattish ledge, cleared the biggest boulders, tied ourselves to the rock and prepared to settle down. Provided the weather held, we had sufficient clothes to survive, but we had only brought food for three meals. The third meal had been lunch, but we still had a couple of tea bags and half a dozen biscuits left over, so we made do with that.

I found my spare socks and put my feet inside my rucksack. With the hood pulled over my face, I snuggled into my down duvet jacket. The stars came out and twinkled in a black night sky while the lights of Chamonix shone safely in the valley below.

We spent a bone shatteringly cold night, sleeping fitfully on the ledge with a drop of well over a thousand feet below us. It was a strange situation: serious to the point of life-threatening, but we had the knowledge and equipment, coupled with the strength and the confidence to get through. It was an adventure and there was no doubt that we would find a way out. Today I find it amusing that neither of us considered it enough of an emergency or were sufficiently hungry to break in to our survival rations!

Unable to sleep we started moving at dawn, shaking the stiffness out of our cold tired limbs. We made a third and fourth cup of tea from the same tea bags and shared a battered orange that I found lurking deep in my bag.

I remember my hands trembling uncontrollably with the cold as we roped up for the start, but as the sun rose there was the most amazing transformation. The rock warmed and the energy began to come back into our bodies, which was as well as the crux of the climb the 'fissure Knubel' is close below the summit.

We reached the aiguille mid-morning and perched on its pinnacle alongside a four-foot iron statue of Notre-Dame de La Salette. We wondered at the view, but our joy was quickly tempered by the prospect of the route down by way of the Nantillons Glacier. We bid 'Our Lady' a fond 'farewell' and began the first of many abseils.

The Nantillons Glacier is nicknamed the 'Englishmen's Graveyard' as its reputation was notorious during the early days of Alpine exploration. The surface is an endless series of yawning crevasses which became a long, boring, zigzag route. It demanded careful concentration at a time when fatigue was setting in and, not surprisingly, we were very hungry.

In mid-afternoon sunshine we finally plodded in to the campsite, tired and aching, but elated after a terrific couple of Alpine days. Babs, a lovely Devon girl, was playing with Gary on the grass. She looked up and smiled.

'Have you had a good time, you two? Would you like a cup of tea?'

'Babs, if only you knew! We had had an absolutely brilliant time.'

21

I Love My Navel

For many years I have enjoyed a quiet and supportive relationship with my navel, my first gift from my mother. Our joy was undisturbed until, one day, a determined and pernicious length of intestine decided to make a bid for freedom and forced a gap through what I once identified as my six-pack. An ugly pale lump, it basked without shame in the Dorset sunshine.

The GP gave it a name, an 'umbilical hernia', and told me to ignore it unless it became a problem. I slowly became resigned to the grand children's amusement at 'granddad's bulgy-belly button'. For the next few years it imposed itself between me and my harmless navel and slowly began to niggle. On 20 February my GP referred me to the specialist and, in time, an appointment arrived for 5 NOVEMBER! Sigh. What should I have expected?

Things began to worsen significantly and it was time, once again to grapple with the exigences of the NHS waiting list.

Our surgery phone line opens at 8am for short notice appointments. I dialled on repeat and eventually got through at 8.03.

'Thank you for calling the… surgery, We are currently experiencing heavy traffic. If you wish to speak to an operative please hold the line. Your call is important to us.'

'Oh yeah?'

'You are number… twenty… in the queue.'

Mozart, loop after interminable loop, but, with a rare stroke of good fortune, I was eventually given an appointment later that day. It took only a brief examination for the GP to tell me to report to Accident and Emergency,

My heart sank to my boots as I recalled my experience twelve months ago when I suffered the eccentricities of the A and E waiting room with a cardiac problem. Could history be repeating itself?

'Don't worry. I'll phone through and tell them you're coming, so the wait shouldn't be too bad.' The GP offered.

'Oh yeah?'

'Thank you for calling A and E, We are currently experiencing heavy traffic. If you wish to speak to an operative please hold the line. Your call is important to us. You are number… eight… in line.'

Mozart.

'Argggghhh!'

Not me, the GP. I was still sunnyside up on the examination couch. But for my painful navel, a smile might have crossed my face at the sight of a hard-working GP experiencing some of the misery that the NHS regularly heaps on his patients.

AFTER 20 MINUTES!

'Hello A and E…'

'Oh, this is Dr… Click… whirr…' And the line went dead. Cut off.

'Argggghhh!'

If 'bedside manner' is the term used to describe the way a medical professional behaves, what followed must have been one of the rarest examples.

No more phone calls, he printed off a large sheaf of notes to take with me. In a huge, angry 'doctor's scrawl' he endorsed the top.

'ATTEMPTED TO PHONE, BUT COULD NOT GET THROUGH AFTER TWENTY MINUTES!'

I went home to ask my wife to drive me in, reflecting on the state of the NHS when a large health centre could not speak to the local A and E department by phone.

'WAITING TIME 2HRS 35MINS'. Despite being well within government targets a familiar air of gloom and resignation pervaded the A and E waiting room. Fortunately my doctor's note greased the wheels and I was given a CT scan and admitted to a ward for observation.

I was examined by a dour and unsmiling consultant. Perhaps you get that way if you spend your working day gazing at other people's navels. My 'strangulated umbilical hernia' was infected and would need surgery. There were two options: treat with anti-biotics. If the infection clears, then consider sending me home and returning, in due course, for planned surgery (back on the NHS waiting list again!). The alternative was emergency surgery as soon as possible.

Could he seriously consider sending me home for maybe weeks to contend with the pain inflicted by that mean and determined length of intestine? Oh, I remember. I have an appointment booked for 5 November. Could we use that?

Before any surgical procedure could take place, certain cardiac medicines that I take had to clear through my system. This would provide a handy twenty-four hours for observation. Meanwhile the ugly, but painless yellow bump that the pernicious intestine previously occupied was now a little smaller than a Victoria plum, a similar colour and throbbing like the speakers at a Stones' concert.

There was no alternative. My 'emergency' procedure was 'planned' for the next day.

The pernicious intestine was sewn back in its rightful place and my waistline once more assumed a regular circumference. After three nights, I was home for lunch on the fourth day.

At last I'm reunited with my faithful old navel, though it might yet benefit from a little cosmetic surgery!

22

The Arms Find

The night was cold and damp and we were nearing the end of a deeply frustrating foot patrol with an informer. It was a high-risk tactic that was often successful, but, this time, we had lifted no one. As we approached the entrance to our base, I decided to cross the road to the chip shop and check the queue waiting to be served. A lad, who we knew to be an active member of the IRA youth organisation, was sitting on the pavement, as teenagers do. The people in the queue looked up nervously.

'What's your name?' I shouted to the lad on the ground.

He mumbled a reply. I swung my leg back, kicked him hard in the thigh and screamed,

'Stand up when I'm talking to you.' A command that he clearly couldn't obey with a dead leg!

In the shadows on the other side of the road a nervous informer was being hustled quickly and quietly through the gate by his minder. I hurriedly left the shop before any trouble could start and went into the Ops Room. By the time I had completed my patrol report the telephone wires on the Northern Ireland complaints hotline were buzzing about the brutality of a British soldier towards a youth queuing for chips in Andersonstown.

***

The following morning at 0450 my four-man patrol gathered at the gate. We loaded and headed off into the estate. I was hoping for an uneventful patrol, quiet and safe before dawn on a Sunday. With little likelihood of any incidents, it should provide an opportunity for a good look round.

On a number of previous occasions, I had noticed that the front door of number 26 Riverdale Park North had been left ajar in the small hours. Often, sympathisers would leave a key on the outside of a door, so that fugitives looking for a safe house could come in and use a bed. This was in the back of my mind.

I was amazed to see that the house had been ravaged by fire and now seemed unoccupied, so I decided to take a closer look. The garage door had been pulled off and was propped over the frame. Bombardier Tolson and I eased it back and revealed a dark blue Morris 1100. We peered cautiously into the car and noticed a number of bundles on the back seat, among them a Post Office mail bag.

You leave well alone in situations like this as the car might contain a booby-trapped bomb, but my mind was racing and curiosity got the better of me. I gently opened a rear door, all the time dreading the small click of a detonator, which might have been the last thing that I heard! I lifted the edge of the mail bag and a quantity of live rounds fell out.

Tolson and I breathed deeply, stepped outside and I reported 'a significant arms find' to Battery Ops. Suddenly we were very vulnerable. The person who had left the arms wouldn't risk being caught in the building with them as it would imply ownership, but they would not have left them unguarded. Probably a sentry's eyes were watching us from a house nearby, so we needed to be alert for a firefight if the IRA decided to defend the cache. Ironically, it never occurred to us that if we had captured their weapons they were unlikely to have anything to shoot at us with!

Search and forensic teams quickly arrived with 5 Troop who established a cordon. The house was empty, but in the back of the car, among many other things we found: ten firearms, including two .303 rifles, a Thompson machine gun, two sawn-off shotguns and an Armalite, over 1400 rounds of ammunition, a British Army hand grenade and two-way radios. Also in the car were the proceeds of a Post Office raid, including Postal Orders that would have been used to pay IRA Volunteers who were on the run and couldn't have normal jobs. It was the biggest single arms find that had been made in Northern Ireland at that time.

Some nights previously I had been on patrol in the estate and heard a strange noise. It had carried a distance on the still night air and was unmistakably the sound of someone digging. Digging at two in the morning – why? We followed the noise, but it stopped before we could discover anything and, it was such a minor event, that I don't think I even included it in my report.

A few days after the find we made a routine search of a house in Riverdale Park Drive and discovered a hole about three feet square and three feet deep in the garden at the rear. The weapons had probably been removed from it the night I had heard digging. My curiosity had captured the whole of E Company's armoury and with one swift slice had cut the nuts off the IRA in our area - for the time being.

The base was buzzing with excitement as the arms find was catalogued. By now it was mid-morning and, tired from the night's activities, I sat in the cookhouse drinking tea with my lads, pleased with our day's work. Colonel Bill sat smiling and laughing and congratulated us on our find. When he stood up to go, he called me outside with him. I knew what was coming.

'Why did you get involved with those kids last night? The GOC was rung by the local MP who received complaints about it. And you risked compromising the informer.

There was no answer. 'I don't know, Colonel, I am very sorry. It won't happen again.'

'Absolutely right, it won't. Will it? Well done with that arms find.'

He slapped me on the shoulder and moved away.

It had to be said and, as always, Colonel Bill hit just the right note.

23

The Revenge of The Pantomime Cow

Brad lay on the bed gazing at the ceiling, his naked body bruised, scratched and bleeding. His successful career was in tatters after it had all been going so well. How had it come to this?

***

As a boy he had excelled at sport playing Rugby for England schools, so Sports Science was an obvious choice for university. He met the course with boundless enthusiasm and, although standards were extremely high, he became a stalwart of the University 1st XV. Confident and noisy, with a flashing smile he was a sporting hero, popular with everyone.

In the disco at the students' union he was captivated by a young 'fresher', a petite girl with sparkling blue eyes. Her name was Rae and their friendship blossomed. In the Easter break they were with the university party that skied in Austria. They shared a passion for high energy activities and in the mountains and snow they fell in love.

He graduated and they spent the long holiday surfing in Cornwall before she returned to university and he began his first teaching job at a school near his home. When she graduated she taught at a school near his and they married during the Christmas break.

Theirs was a hectic sporting lifestyle. Through the winter Brad captained his local rugby club and was a regular selection for the County side. Rae belonged to the town netball club and helped at a friend's dance school. At Easter they skied in the Alps and in the long summer holidays they surfed the giant waves on the French Atlantic coast.

They were now together at a large Comprehensive school where he was head of sport and she taught dance and drama. In their forties, they were a successful couple who enjoyed a busy life.

Theirs looked a perfect marriage, but underneath a crack was beginning to appear. In the hectic early years, starting a family was not a priority, but, as time passed, Rae began to long for children. The first time she broached the subject, Brad tenderly rejected it as 'not the right time'.

Each time she mentioned children his rejection was harsher and more insensitive until it began to be brutal and unkind. Rae was seeing traits in him that she didn't like. Signs of egotism, chauvinism and narcissism were driving a wedge between them.

Now she was approaching the menopause and, with her body clock racing, she was acutely aware that time was running out.

The male menopause affected him in several ways. He had accepted that his proper place was now in the club 2nd XV where he could revel in his past reputation, but there were a number of obvious signs of his resistance to the inevitable.

He'd suddenly lost his greying temples and his hair became an unconvincing brown. A bottle of Grecian 2000 lurked behind his shaving foam. Parked in front of their four-bedroom suburban detached was a macho black four-by-four with tinted windows. He was fighting a losing battle.

***

Under Brad's influence sport at the school was strong, but he was always keen to raise standards. One of the school's short-comings was that hockey was played on grass and didn't promote the speed and skills of the modern game. He felt they needed a new astro-turf pitch.

His view was shared by his deputy, Brenda Bilston, who had, in her time, been a formidable hockey goal keeper. Nearing retirement, Brenda was now about five feet by four feet with short cropped grey hair. Her square jaw was marked with a number of moles that appeared to have piano wire growing from them.

Together, they put the case to the head who wholeheartedly agreed, but the project would require fund-raising.

Christmas was approaching and planning was underway for one of the most eagerly anticipated events of the school year, the staff pantomime. It was an immensely popular event when they happily made fools of themselves in front of all and sundry. A huge audience was anticipated, which would give a healthy lift to the hockey pitch fund.

This year's production was 'Jack and the Beanstalk'. Brad and Rae regularly took part, but it had taken a little persuasion to convince him that Daisy the Cow was a comedy role tailor-made for the two of them.

Rehearsals were going well and the cast had been fitted for costumes, but there was a problem. The costume for Daisy the Cow was grubby and torn and was plainly unsatisfactory. The agency agreed to supply a replacement, but it was late in arriving.

Rae was chatting in the staff room with George Maxwell an elderly maths teacher. 'Max' had a fascination for conjuring and every year a special part for 'Max the Magician was written into the pantomime.

He placed a plastic cup from the drinking fountain over a coin on the table. A silk handkerchief appeared from nowhere and settled over the cup. He whisked it away and, hey presto! The coin was gone. Rae laughed happily. Max did two more similar tricks.

'That's brilliant, Max. Your so clever. I do wish I knew how you did it.'

'Oh. it's easy when you know the secret. I've been doing this for years. Every week, as a boy, I'd take my pocket money to the Magic Emporium in the High Street and buy a new trick.'

'Really?'

'Yes, the shop's still going and I'm popping in tomorrow. You're welcome to come along, if you're interested.'

'Oh, Max, I'd love to.'

The next day, after school she met Max in the High Street. The Magic Emporium was a place from a bygone era. Costumes, false limbs, masks, wands and all manner of paraphernalia hung from the walls. On a trestle were two boxes. used to saw the lady in half. There were stink bombs, floating sugar, whoopy cushions, all sorts of novelties and shelves stacked with dozens of conjuring tricks. She watched in awe as Max opened the boxes and explained how the tricks were done.

When it was time to go, she thanked him profusely for the fascinating visit and drove home, her mind buzzing with the things she'd seen.

On the day before the performance a box containing Daisy the Cow's costume finally arrived. In it were two pairs of trousers, with elasticated waists and ankles, and the body with the head attached.

Rae admired it and noticed that unlike the cotton fabric of the old costume the new one was made of a heavy fleece material. Presumably the designer thought it bore closer resemblance to a real cow! It was going to be hot - very hot and needed careful consideration. A wicked plan began to take shape in her mind.

After school she drove into town and parked outside the Magic Emporium. She slipped round to the shelves to where the tricks were displayed and took two packets from a box next to the stink bombs. She paid for them and drove home.

Brad had been on an away fixture with the school basketball team so wouldn't see the new costume until the day of the performance. When he got home she enthused over it, describing every detail.

'There's one thing we must think about. That fleece is so thick that we're going to cook inside it. We'll have to wear the absolute minimum.'

'Really?'

'Yes, really, the absolute minimum. The most would be your swimming stuff.'

'OK, I'll give it some thought.'

***

The dressing room was a hive of activity as everyone got ready. Brad was shocked by the weight of the trousers, she was right, they were going to be uncomfortably hot.

'Absolute minimum' was the instruction, so he'd taken her at her word. He'd rejected his normal swim shorts and dug deep in the drawer to find the old pair of Speedos he'd worn as a twenty-year-old. Now he struggled to heave them over his thighs and cram the rest of his body into them. His menopausal mindset had refused to acknowledge how much his shape had changed. They were tight, very tight – indecently tight.

Don't worry. No one will see. He pulled on the trousers, found the body and joined Rae in the wings.

Meanwhile the audience was arriving.

Brenda was happy to be front of house as she was never a thespian, a word like it, but not quite 'thespian'. For the first half she stood at the door as the 'greeter', welcoming the guests in her bullet proof tweed suit and shiny brown brogues. The VIP party arrived.

'Good evening headmaster.' She nodded, smiling at the others.

With the Head were the Chairman of Governors and a tubby little man with a florid complexion, bulging eyes and several chins. He was a local entrepreneur whose friendship the Chairman was vigorously courting in the hope that he might be the generous benefactor needed to support the hockey pitch fund.

His wife was much younger. 'Blowsy' was a kind description. A high hemline and low neckline are rarely an indication of class and, with her 'belle decolletage', she made Dolly Parton look sophisticated. They took their seats in the front row, the lights dimmed and the show began.

***

The audience were soon rocking with laughter at Daisy's star role, but inside the heavy costume all was not well. Rae was right, it was unbearably hot and Brad was bathed is sweat.

The itch you can't scratch is an unimaginable Chinese torture. It started with a tickle on his shoulder. He rubbed it against the heavy fleece, but it persisted. Then an elbow, more rubbing, but it moved to his ribs and the itching intensified.

He released a hand from Rae's waist and began to scratch vigorously, to no avail. It was getting worse. His whole body was on fire and he had to scratch.

The audience were laughing, as the front half of Daisy continued with the carefully choreographed moves while the middle and rear began to jump and jiggle inexplicably. Was it comic improvisation? Could there be something wrong with Daisy's rear half?

Inside the costume Brad was becoming frantic. Every inch of his body burned. In desperation he threw off the suit. There, under the spotlight for all to see, he stood scratching, scratching, SCRATCHING.

In desperation he hurled his cow pants away and clawed at his painful knees. The discarded garment flew gracefully through the air and finally alighted round the eyes of the generous benefactor.

Thus he was protected from the undignified sight of a well-built man in indecent Speedos running, rolling and leaping, unable to satisfy a relentless urge to scratch. The performance was halted and the audience gasped in disbelief.

During the interval Brenda's place was at the front with a large tray of ice creams and she was moving forward as Brad's problems unfolded. Eager to help a friend in trouble, she rapidly despatched the tray with an off-load than an All Black would have been proud of, then rushed the stage.

Unfortunately, the Chairman of Governors was no All Black. He missed the catch and the flying tray struck him full in the face. On the floor he twitched like a stunned mullet. The contents of the tray departed their erstwhile home and flew in a gentle arc towards the generous benefactor's wife where, with a splat, they came to rest.

The belle decolletage was decorated with a thick layer of raspberry ripple that bestowed on a previously vulgar item, a degree of taste.

Brenda hit Brad with a flying tackle that drove him into the ancient back curtain. She grappled on the floor trying desperately to stop his manic scratching. She pinned his arms to his sides, but her bullet proof tweeds only worsened the problem.

The ancient back curtain finally departed from its mooring and filled the air with choking dust. The heavy fabric covered the struggling couple, together with a bevy of extras dressed as Bavarian maidens with painted rosy circles on their cheeks.

Under the curtain Brenda finally achieved a submission hold on Brad. With her arms locked in a fierce bear hug round his naked torso she was experiencing strange new feelings that she'd never known before. She began to wonder if, after all these years, she had been wrong about her sexual orientation.

The Design and Technology teacher, who was running the audio-visuals, was convulsed with a sudden asthma attack and, in his rush to escape the dust cloud, he knocked the control console to the floor in a shower of sparks. The stage lights fused and the audio system jumped to the next loop.

On the dimly lit stage humps rose and fell under the ancient back curtain in a surreal image of an angry sea as those trapped under it tried to escape, all to the accompaniment of a rich baritone reciting.

'Fee Fi Fo Fum, I smell the blood of an Englishman.'

The close observer would have noticed that through it all, the front half of Daisy stood, quietly watching from the side. Now the figure seemed to be trembling. Inside the costume Rae shuddered with laughter.

In the front row, the no-longer generous benefactor stepped over the still prostrate Chairman and finally untangled himself from the cow's trousers. He drew himself up to his full five feet two. His red face was now puce and his bulging eyes threatened to pop from their sockets in anger. His wailing wife's tears melted salty channels through the raspberry ripple as they trickled down the belle decolletage.

The Head gasped as he surveyed the scene. In painful disbelief, he watched his hopes for the hockey pitch disappearing into thin air.

***

Rae drove the four-by-four home with Brad still in shock.

As she removed her make up in the bathroom mirror a smile crossed her lips, a wicked, vindictive smile, a smile of supreme satisfaction. She lifted her handbag from the shelf by the basin and took out the two empty packets that she had bought in the Magic Emporium and dropped them in the loo. She smiled again as the words 'ITCHING POWDER' disappeared into the eternity of the sewers. Evidence destroyed.

Brad lay on his back, his naked body pink with a coating of calamine lotion. She snuggled close.

The skilled interrogator relies on the subject being well softened before beginning the brain washing procedure. Brad was ready.

She placed her head on his shoulder and slid her fingers gently across his chest.

'Don't worry, darling. I still love you.'

He wrapped his arm around her in response.

'We'll get over it. We can start again.

Wouldn't it be nice if we had a little one to help us along the way?'

24

The Golden Screwdriver

Like all couples, Darren and Sharon often had little rows, but rarely fell out like this. It began weeks ago and seemed to be dragging on for ever.

One afternoon a rusty old banger had arrived unexpectedly on a low loader. It seemed Darren had bought it on impulse from a local garage forecourt and it now sat in pieces in his shed. For him, it was a rare opportunity to restore a wonderful classic car. For Sharon, it was savings that could have been better used improving the house. It posed a seemingly intractable problem.

Their son, Grayson loved working with his dad and had spent all Saturday with Darren, while his mum went shopping on her own, then bustled round the house with a face like thunder.

When Darren lay under the car working Grayson would hand him the spanners that he asked for. Now he was working on the engine and could find his own tools, so hands in pockets, Grayson walked round the car admiring it.

The tyres were perished, a bumper was missing, there was rust everywhere and a hundred other things that needed fixing. But beneath it all he could imagine the lovely little car that it would be when dad had restored it to its former glory. He began to understand why dad had so much affection for it.

Noticing his boredom Darren gave him his tin of odd screws and bolts to look at, along with his favourite screwdriver. It was the one his elder brother Malcom had given him for Christmas. Grayson liked his Uncle Malcolm. He was always good for a Werthers Original.

He rolled the screwdriver in his hand. Its lacquered handle was smooth and tactile and sat neatly in his palm. He delighted in the easy way the thread of the bolts moved through the nuts.

A stentorian cry interrupted him.

'DARRRENNN, dinner's ready!' Mum had a monster sad on.

Head down, Grayson trooped into the house behind dad.

'Look at the oil on your hands and that boy's got grease all over his face.'

They washed in silence at the kitchen sink then sat at the table.

The family meal had NOT been made with love and affection. A great, glutinous glob of brown stew struggled off the ladle then fell with splat on to Grayson's plate. A solid, round, grey lump followed it. He loved dumplings but Nelson could have used this one as a cannon ball. He pushed his food round his plate eating little.

After dinner, in an effort at family unity, they watched TV together until it was time for bed. Uncle Malcolm's screw driver fell out of his pocket as he put on his pyjamas. He picked it up and rolled the smooth handle in his palm once more. Mum was coming upstairs. He quickly slid it under his pillow.

The phone rang as mum was finishing his story, so she rushed away.

‘Hello Doreen… Fine thank you…’

It was Auntie Doreen. Those two could talk for Dorset. For what seemed ages they chatted about Uncle Malcolm and Auntie Doreen’s forthcoming wedding. Meanwhile his tummy rumbled with hunger.

He slipped quietly downstairs and found some stilton in the fridge. He cut a slice and, with a couple of cracker biscuits, sneaked back up.

Mum frowned when she noticed the crumbs on the bedside table.

‘What’ve you been eating?’

‘Nothing, mum.’

‘What are those crumbs over there?’

‘I was ever so hungry mum and I only had some cheese and a couple of crackers, honest.’

Her heart melted.

‘Now, you know you shouldn’t eat cheese before bed. It’ll give you a tummy ache and you’ll have nightmares.’

She kissed him good night. With his head on the pillow he reached under and felt the comforting shape of Uncle Malcolm’s screwdriver and before long he was dozing off.

He was woken by a raging pain in his tummy. He winced.

A strong wind parted the curtains and a golden moonbeam shone down on his bed. He blinked in disbelief as he saw a tiny golden fairy creep silently through the window and sit at the top of the moonbeam.

Over her shoulder was a tiny golden satchel. She swished down the moonbeam and landed on her bottom on his duvet, then jumped off the bed and danced out on to the landing. He followed her with his eyes. She paused at his parents' bedroom door then slipped inside. Unable to contain his curiosity, he forgot his tummy ache and tip-toed after her.

She hopped up on to the bed where mum and dad were sleeping and sat on the cobra tattooed on dad's shoulder. From her golden satchel she took a tiny golden purse of fairy dust and sprinkled it into dad's ear. She skipped across to mum and did the same then leaped down to the floor. He rushed back to his room and pulled the duvet up under his chin. His tummy began to hurt again.

The tiny golden fairy sprang on to his bed. Squinting through a half-closed eye, he watched her draw back the covers and undo the bottom button of his pyjama jacket. Then she opened her golden satchel and took out a tiny golden screwdriver, placed it in his navel and began to gently turn it. Seconds later she bent down and lifted out a tiny golden screw which she placed carefully on the bedside table. From the golden satchel she took out a tiny golden aerosol. Still squinting hard, he could just make out the word 'WD40'. The tiny golden fairy gave three short squirts into his navel where the screw had been.

The aerosol was cold and his involuntary shiver startled her. Thinking he was about to wake, she hurriedly threw the golden screwdriver and the golden aerosol into her golden satchel, scurried up the golden moon beam and was gone.

He was woken next morning by a welcoming shaft of sunlight. From downstairs came the sound of mum, singing happily as she made breakfast. Dad was bumping round helping her. Obviously the dramas with the old car had been forgotten.

His tummy problem seemed to have cleared up, but he felt troubled by something that had happened in the night. It was something strange, but he had no clear recollection. He still didn't feel quite right. Perhaps it had all been a dream.

He swung his legs out of bed, yawned and stretched.

He cautiously stood up…

and his arse fell off.

25

Revival

She was dead. At eighty-five the heart attack was hardly a surprise, but the shock was profound. They were childhood sweethearts who had married soon after he left medical school. A brief honeymoon in Bournemouth marked the beginning of a long and happy marriage. Occasionally they would make a sentimental return and it became a special place.

His career progressed and he became a Hospital Consultant. She continued teaching and was eventually the head of a large Primary School.

Retirement had been comfortable and busy with volunteering, hobbies and the occasional cruise, but now she was gone. His family rallied and supported him through the funeral. Her affairs were tied up. Sadly, it was time to draw a line in the sand and move on. There was only one place from which to start.

The sun shone through the window as he awoke in his East Cliff hotel room. He drew back the curtains and smelled the fresh sea air that had given him a sound night's sleep. A bright summer's day beckoned with a dazzling vista over a sparkling blue sea. His spirits were lifted.

He savoured a leisurely breakfast then ambled down to the sea front. On a whim, he stepped on to the beach, removed his shoes and socks and wriggled his toes in the warm sand. Then, with a mixture of guilt and embarrassment, he rolled up his trousers and stepped into the shallows. The water caressed his ankles and he smiled at the long-forgotten feeling as his feet sank into the sand and the waves receded.

He leaned on the rail of the pier and admired the view. Children played on the sand, others frolicked in the sea and bikini clad mums were kissed by the sun. All around was happiness.

Raised voices intruded on his reverie. A man and a woman were arguing loudly. The noises came from behind the amusement arcade. A baby was involved. Things were worsening with threats of violence. His pace quickened as the voices grew steadily angrier.

He rounded the corner and encountered a small, garishly dressed man, wielding a large stick. A woman and baby appeared to be dead.

'That's the way to do it. That's the way to do it. Oh dear, the crocodile has eaten the sausages.'

He found a seat in the warm sunshine, sat back and enjoyed the show.

26

Skiing with Henry

We stepped out of the mini-bus into a swirling misty snow storm. A couple of degrees below zero, the typical wet-snow conditions of south Norway.

I was accompanying a Nordic Ski-Touring Course on a day when the lesson to be taught was emergency snow shelters and survival. The course members were all competent at Nordic skiing and were led by Henry, one of our most experienced instructors.

Henry was a Scot, small, slightly built and incredibly fit. He had spent two years attached to the German Army Alpine School and completed his Alpine Guides Carnet. He was a 'Bergführer', one of the most highly regarded qualifications in mountaineering.

The course was based at Hovden, a popular resort in South Norway with hundreds of kilometres of prepared ski tracks. These tracks varied in length, but were always clearly marked with coloured poles about three metres high.

Henry intended to follow a track for about two kilometres before striking off, uphill for a short distance, to an area where he would teach the lesson.

As we followed the gently rising track the wind became stronger and the snow storm heavier. We battled on, eventually leaving the track and heading more steeply uphill. We were in driving snow and near whiteout, but despite this we continued. Coping with difficult conditions was an essential part of the course.

We reached a stage where visibility was so poor that we couldn't see the humps or hollows in front of us and it was obvious that we couldn't continue. Despite the fact that we were not far from a main road and civilization we were in a very serious situation.

Fortunately, we found a depression in the snow, which was probably a small stream bed, took off our skis and placed our rucksacks in two lines. Henry then found his Zdarsky Sack, which was like a tent with no poles and functioned as a group survival shelter. We sat opposite each other on our rucksacks and threw the sack over us, tucking the edges under our feet. A couple of skis were used as tent poles to keep the shelter up.

Out of the biting wind and with the heat of our bodies warming the Zdarsky Sack, we cheerfully found our flasks and sandwiches and had lunch. Things were fine, but we still had a lot to do to get to safety.

I looked at Henry. He finished eating and I noticed that he carefully left a sandwich and his chocolate bar, just in case things went wrong and he needed it later. It was an old soldier's trick, something that I always did.

Lunch over, Henry briefed the group. It would be dangerous for anyone to become separated so it was important we stayed close together and kept an eye on the person behind as well as the person in front. We re-packed our sacks, then quickly folded the Zdarsky Sack and found our skis.

Henry led, carefully following his compass, while I brought up the rear, watching my compass as a double check. Conditions were appalling and we kept falling as it was impossible to judge the terrain in the flat light. On one occasion I fell backwards and when I got to my feet, I was facing the wrong way. There was a brief moment of panic when I couldn't see the others, until I turned and glimpsed them trudging on through the gloom.

We had probably skied about a kilometre when we found the blue poles that marked the track and were able to follow them home. When the minibus eventually emerged from the gloom we were mighty relieved and gathered round, laughing and joking. Still full of adrenalin, we finished our flasks.

The emergency snow shelters lesson would have to be taught another day, but the group had gained valuable practical experience of dealing with extreme weather conditions.

Henry sat alone and smiled. I watched him open his rucksack and eat his last sandwich, his acknowledgement that we were safe again.

27

Ice Cream For All

Not everyone enjoys an Indian summer.

September, it was unbearably hot in the sandbagged sangar that stood on a platform six feet above and to the left of the main gate. The two-hour sentry duty was boring. They watched an ice cream van approach and negotiate the speed bumps.

Footsteps on the ladder, he was huge, so tall his beret brushed the underside of the roof. In his younger days he'd boxed heavyweight and his face bore evidence of his presence in the darker areas of the scrum. The lads knew him as the Jolly Green Giant. The Battery Sergeant Major announced his presence in his usual booming manner.

'Who've we got here then? Bloody hell, Webby, lift him up. He'll never see over the sand bags.'

Gunner Webb smiled. His mate, Gunner Bennet, was the smallest man in the battery. Minimum height for the army was five foot two. Bennet only made it in thick wool socks.

In the distance they heard the chimes of the ice cream van.

'I could murder an ice cream.'

'Yeah, one or two others out there I could murder as well.'

They laughed. Despite the difference in rank the banter continued. They loved it and the BSM knew it kept spirits up.

‘Who’s out at the moment, sir?

‘Dinger’s up at North End. Haven’t heard anything from him, though.’

Almost on cue a volley of shots rang out from the distance.

‘This is six one, contact, wait out.’ From Bombardier Bell.

The BSM was already on his way to the Ops Room.

‘At: 1115… From: area numbers 22, 23 North End Road… Eight high velocity rounds… At: my call sign… Ten rounds returned… Am following up.’

The reserve troop roared out the gate, but the gunmen were long gone. Two men had walked briskly away from North End Road to the clothes they had hidden in a black bag behind a row of garages. A quick change, into their stolen car and, in no time, they were in Ballymurphy joking with their colleagues.

The sun beat down as the soldiers knocked on doors asking the occupants if they’d seen anything. It seemed the whole street was visually impaired. An old couple walked by. No one was above suspicion.

‘Good morning, sir. Do you have any ID?

The old man looked away as Dinger checked his details. Then he looked him square in the eye.

‘Get yerself an ice cream, sonny, an ICE CREAM.’

‘Yeah, uh, sure. Thank you, sir.’

He moved on wondering what he meant.

He was filling in the patrol report when the BSM walked in.

'How's it going, Bom? What happened?'

'Oh, we were moving along North End, sir. A couple of hoods took a pop at us from between the houses. They're using Armalites, we found the shell cases. Fired half a dozen rounds and bugged out. Same as before.'

'That's the third time this week. Just as well the Paddys are crap shots.'

His language hid his concern. Sooner or later someone would be hit.

Sweat trickled down Reg Lewis's face. His heavy flak jacket prevented the air from circulating round his body and made things more unbearable. Two days had passed, but the fine weather was lasting.

Bing-bong, bing-bong. The ice cream man was still taking advantage of the sunshine.

CRACK, CRACK… CRACK, CRACK. Reg and his patrol dived for cover and returned fire.

Dinger Bell's patrol was in a different area and heard the shots. Instinctively they began running to Reg's aid, panting in the heat.

Now the ice cream van was coming towards them… towards them, but not at the normal sedate speed. The ice cream man had his foot on the floor boards.

'Get yerself an ice cream, sonny, an ICE CREAM.'

Instinctively, Dinger jumped into the road waving him down. Brakes screeching, the van swerved and collided with a lamp post.

The driver was slumped over the wheel. Dinger wrenched the door open, dragged him out and slammed his face against the side of the van.

'Hands against the van. Feet back, FEET BACK! Dan, cover him. Ray, pat him down.'

The patrol ran in. The back of the van was a jumble of boxes and cartons, the air filled with the sweet smell of confectionary. But Dinger sensed more. Beneath the counter was a dirty towel. He pulled it back to reveal two Armalite rifles. He savoured the aroma of cordite and rifle oil.

'OK, sunshine. You're in deep shit.'

More troops arrived. Hands zip-tied, the ice cream man was bundled into the back of a Saracen. He was sweating hard and shaking. Dinger's boys smiled at him and said nothing.

The ice cream van was still driveable, so followed on with two soldiers in the front, one, with his weapon out of the window, smiling at passers-by.

A Military Police team and others were waiting in camp to check the vehicle. The ice cream man stood at the rear to witness the search. His takings were counted, the weapons were bagged and he signed an acknowledgement. He was taken away for questioning.

The Battery Commander thanked the search teams and they departed. Standing by the back of the vehicle the BSM flicked the lid off one of the ice cream tubs and dipped a finger in.

'Mmm, good stuff this, sir. Be a shame to let it go to waste.'

'It certainly would Sergeant Major. It certainly would.'

He smiled, turned on his heel and left.

***

When Dinger came in for his dinner the Jolly Green Giant stood at the end of the hatch, a huge serving spoon in his hand. In front of him were three large metal bowls of ice cream. A cardboard notice read

'A PRESENT FROM DINGER'.

The lads laughed and gave him a cheer.

He didn't stay long. He was back on patrol at 1930. As he walked the same streets the old man was in his garden. His wife drew back from the window as the patrol approached.

He looked Dinger in the eye.

'Did ye enjoy yer ice cream, sonny?'

'Aye, we certainly did, dad. We certainly did. Thank you.'

The old man smiled and went back to his flowers.

They'd found the weapons and bagged the courier, but the gunmen were still out there. Sooner or later they would be re-armed.

28

My Prostate and I

My prostate and I have enjoyed an active and energetic life, leaping tall buildings and peeing over high walls. Sadly, all good things come to an end.

My father euphemistically referred to it as 'the old man's problem' when he reported to Casualty one afternoon. He was sent home and told.

'Drink plenty of water and it will blast through.'

It didn't. Three hours later he had a rapid run back to the hospital doubled up in an ambulance. He told me that the subsequent operation was 'like being pulled through with red hot barbed wire.' Aged about forty, I winced and put my father's problem to the back of my mind.

In the winter of 2021 I was in hospital overnight after an operation on my neck. I was told I would be released when my 'bodily functions' returned to normal. I stretched the truth when I went to the loo and was marked fit to go home. Nothing more happened and by 6pm I was in severe pain. My prostate had locked on to my ureter with a grip like the Boston Strangler. By the time I reached A and E, I was in such pain that I didn't notice the sign at reception saying 'WAITING TIME 4 HOURS.

Fortunately, my screams of agony beat the clock and I found myself lying on a hospital bed gazing at my distended abdomen, hoping, one day, to be able to see my toes again. The feeling of relief was indescribable, as a bag by the bed filled to the size of a small Zeppelin. I was sent home with a catheter.

Dejected, I reflected on how I had gone in to hospital as a neck patient and come out as a prostate patient. I hoped these problems didn't come in threes.

In truth, I had been aware of my 'old man's problem' for some time, but was keen to get other medical difficulties resolved first, so had ignored it.

A few days later a health visitor came to the house and removed the catheter to see if the problem had righted itself. It hadn't and hours later she returned to replace it. I was referred to a specialist.

When I presented in pain to Casualty my problem was acute and required immediate attention. The NHS attitude now was that the catheter was a long-term solution. I could soldier on, waiting indefinitely for an operation.

Living with a catheter is neither easy nor pleasant. The tap mechanism is a push fit and was occasionally dislodged by careless movement. Strenuous activities, like digging and lifting, caused bleeding, made worse by my cardiac medicines. Public toilets and the regular catheter changes by the kind and understanding health visitors were embarrassing and undignified. Unwilling to wait for treatment beyond the age of a hundred, I decided to seek private help.

A fresh-faced Registrar interviewed me to discuss the outcome of a CT scan. He flashed up a monitor and pointed gleefully at the shiny image of my two hip replacements, reflecting the scanner's rays. Below and between them was an ominous black circle that was my prostate.

'Normally the prostate is the size of a walnut. Yours is about the size of an orange.'

I had no ambition to achieve an entry in the Guinness Book of Records.

He suggested several surgical options. I scanned the room nervously, for signs of my father's barbed wire. The procedure he recommended was 'prostatic embolization' in which an incision is made in the femoral artery and a tube is directed through to the blood vessels in the prostate which are constricting the ureter. A solution containing thousands of microscopic plastic beads is injected; these block the blood supply, shutting down blood flow to the area and effectively killing the cells. It was quick, with minimal pain, so I agreed to it.

Weeks later I was admitted for the operation, during which I would be conscious, but sedated. Monitors were rigged above the operating table showing a live x-ray of my abdomen which the doctors would use to conduct the procedure. In my drowsy state I lay back to enjoy the show. The room was cool with calming music. All involved worked with quiet efficiency. I was very impressed.

In due course the senior doctor told me that he was finished and it had gone well. He handed over to the nursing team to return me to the ward.

A trolley was brought alongside the operating table. On it was a stiff plastic sheet with holes round the edges that would act as handles. It would be slid under me on the table and I would be lifted on it on to the trolley.

Three people reached over me and rolled me on my side. A team opposite pushed the plastic under me and I was slid into the middle of it.

The teams took their positions and I lay admiring what had, so far, been another efficient team effort.

They all looked at the senior person.

'On my command lift… lift.'

As I was raised I let out an ear-piercing shriek. The lift was halted with me six inches above the table. Concentrating on the main task, someone had forgotten to unhook my bag from the table and I was still attached by my catheter which was tugging on the part of my body through which it entered! Back in the ward I wiped the tears from my eyes.

I was sent home with a warning that there would be some pain for 24 hours while my body adjusted.

Indeed there was and, as the pain killers wore off, it felt like sitting on a fiery ants' nest. I consoled myself that it was infinitely better than my father's experience with the red-hot barbed wire.

Days later, to my relief, the kindly health visitor removed my last catheter. We didn't throw a party, but I was delighted to be almost back to normal.

Today, I am no longer eager to leap tall buildings or pee over high walls. My prostate and I are happy to enjoy a quiet retirement.

29

The Two-Part Snake

In the seventies, Gunner recruits from Woolwich were taught basic fieldcraft skills in a picturesque area of streams and woodland deep in the Kent countryside. For a week they operated from a patrol base and slept under 'bashas' that they made using their waterproof ponchos.

They had been given the explanation and demonstration and had been left on their own for imitation and practice.

The staff were about a hundred yards away in the admin area when two of the recruits approached with a third, who was holding his right arm across his chest. The casualty was Gunner Newton from Manchester, a typical recruit, tall and skinny with greasy fair hair, a pasty complexion and terminal acne.

'Yes?' Growled Charlie Lewis, the Troop Staff Sergeant.

'Excuse me, Staff, Newton's bin bit.'

'What by?'

'We were clearing some twigs and stuff and there was a snake lying underneath, so Newton picked it up to look at it and the snake bit him.' Newton looked at the ground sheepishly.

Resisting the temptation to ask how the snake was, Lewis replied.

'What? Form a posse and hunt down that snake. I want it dead or alive. On second thoughts, I want it dead.'

Outside Britain it is sometimes useful to take the dead snake with the casualty so that the doctors can be certain to administer the correct medicine. Since the adder is the only venomous snake in Britain this is not normally necessary, nor is it usual to form a posse in Kent.

Adders have since been protected so this would now be against the law.

The two recruits ran back to the patrol base while Lewis went to find a Land Rover and I looked at Newton's hand. His right thumb was swelling and two clear puncture marks from the venomous fangs were reddening. He had obviously been bitten by an adder and needed to go to hospital quickly. Adder bites are rarely fatal so I was not unduly concerned. We were getting Newton into the Land Rover when his two mates came running back, this time carrying a small cardboard box that had previously contained a twenty-four-hour ration.

'We got the snake, Staff.'

'You what? Let's have a look.' Making sure he wasn't standing too close.

Inside the box was a lovely little adder, about fourteen inches long, plump, beautifully coloured and dead... seriously dead.

I have always maintained that a soldier can repair anything in the world, from a nuclear submarine to a deck chair, if he has three basic essentials, a roll of two-inch black masking tape, a trip flare picket and some Don Ten signals cable.

Because the snake had bitten their friend Newton, they attacked it with 'shovels infantry' and, so that it couldn't bite anyone else, they continued hitting it until it was cut in two.

In this instance, to make the repair they needed only the first of the three essentials, the black masking tape. So that the snake would look its best for the hospital staff, they had joined its two halves with a two-inch-wide strip.

Lewis took the box and drove Newton to the casualty department of the local hospital. Two smiling nurses called them into a treatment cubicle.

'Now, what's the problem?'

'He's been bitten by a poisonous snake.'

'And how do YOU know it was poisonous?' was the slightly pompous reply.

'Because I've got it here.'

He opened the box and tipped the dead adder, resplendent in its two inches of black masking tape, on to the floor. It was some time before the two nurses could be coaxed down from their perch on top of a steel locker to treat Newton's wound.

Newton needed to be kept under observation and was led away to one of the wards for pain killers and anti-biotics. About an hour later Lewis was shown in to see him. He lay propped up on pillows, trying hard not to appear smug at the prospect of a night in a warm hospital rather than out under the stars.

'Right, lad, I'll bring in your washing and shaving kit and, while I'm at it, I'll fetch your poncho and poles so that you can make a basha over there in the corner of the ward.'

Newton smiled weakly as a recruit is never too sure when an instructor is joking.

30

Taff Thomas

Lieutenant Richard Balshaw was apprehensive. Unusual for him, but he had a nagging suspicion that the locals had wised up to the tactics they would use on the patrol he was about to lead. He pulled on his combat jacket and checked his equipment in readiness.

Two vehicles would cruise the area. Balshaw with Bombardier Nichol and Gunner Thomas would form a snatch squad, lightly dressed and equipped, each armed with a 9mm pistol and baton. Balshaw would be peering through the optics in the turret of the Saracen. When he identified a suspect, they would bale out at top speed and apprehend him. The suspect would be bundled into the vehicle and driven off for questioning.

At 1020 the vehicles were driving slowly through the streets, being pelted with stones and bottles. A group of youths stood on a street corner. One was a known activist. He shouted above the engine noise.

'Right. Street corner. Three men. Target is green shirt blue jeans.'

Nichol and Taff Thomas were in the seats by the doors. Balshaw slammed his hand on the driver's shoulder.

'HALT, ACTION!'

Everything was happening at once. The snatch squad jumped out and charged towards the three men. Two fled left, green-shirt ran up an alley between the houses, followed by Balshaw's squad.

Suddenly gunmen opened up at the rear of the Saracen as the remainder were crashing out. Gunner Andrews swung the wheel and slewed it across the line of fire. Mercifully no one was hurt. He and Ford were left inside, firing through the weapon ports.

In the alley, green-shirt slipped through a side gate. A gunman appeared from another gate, fired four quick shots and was gone. Balshaw went down, screaming, his femur shattered above the knee. Desperate to stem the bleeding, Nichol jammed a field dressing in the wound and bound it tight, then ran back down the alley, leaving Thomas to carry on.

In the street the gun fight was continuing. The rest of the patrol were pinned down in the gardens. The two soldiers were still firing from inside the Saracen with rounds pinging off the body. Nichol caught Ford's eye and frantically beckoned. He got the message and as Andrews reversed, Ford guided him.

With Nichol at the shoulders and Thomas lifting his legs they dragged Balshaw to the end of the alley. Bullets cracked around them as they crossed the gap and he was pulled into the vehicle.

Nichol thrust his pistol into Ford's hand, grabbed Ford's rifle and dropped down behind a wall where Gunner Barnes was pinned down. The Saracen roared off.

Nichol looked at Barnes.

'Give me covering fire'

As Barnes fired he dashed forward to the next garden. Barnes leap-frogged past him in the same way. It was a cue for pairs on the other side of the road to do likewise. The firing suddenly stopped and the troops charged, but the gunmen had fled.

***

After the morning's incident the mood was sombre and subdued. Balshaw had lost a lot of blood and was in intensive care. The BSM walked into the MT yard. He found Thomas and Andrews cleaning out the back of the Saracen.

'How's it going, lads?' He said quietly

'OK thanks, sir.' Neither looked up.

Taff was trying to remove signs of blood from a join in the deck plates, at the same time, subconsciously wiping it from his memory. The sounds would be more difficult to erase.

'You two did a great job this morning – excellent. There's not much doubt you saved his life.'

Taff Thomas looked up, but he couldn't find the words.

'We always knew something like this might happen. It hits us all hard, but there's nothing we can do about it. We've just got to keep going and put these bastards behind bars where they belong.' He stayed talking with them for about twenty minutes.

***

At 1900 Bombardier Nichol was walking the streets again. Taff was part of the patrol. People were out, women blowing whistles and jeering. Stones from all sides. Then the chants.

'The British soldier's got one leg. Doo dah, doo dah. The British soldier's got one leg.

Doo dah, doo dah day.'

Nichol took a step up the path towards the group. Then thought better of it. The anger burned inside him. They walked on.

They followed a group of stone-throwing youths down a cul-de-sac. They were in front of a row of garages, goading, provoking, pushing things to the limit. Taff made eye contact with a lad of about eighteen. He was, jeering, calling him on.

Jaw set in fury, he stepped up and slammed the youth's shoulder against the garage, his left forearm pressing hard on his Adam's apple. He let go and brought his right elbow up behind his rifle butt and smashed him under the ear. As he crumpled, he punched him repeatedly with his left fist.

Nichol had seen it all and ran in.

'That's enough. Enough. Pack it in. Leave him.'

He eventually pulled Thomas away. A crowd had gathered, screaming with anger and indignation. They fought their way out with rubber bullets and in an hour were back in camp.

The BSM was waiting, stern faced.

'Brigade has been on the phone. The complaints line is red hot. A soldier beat up a lad on our patch. What do you know about it?'

'That's probably us sir. Taff had a set-to with a lad who was giving us trouble.'

'Is that right Thomas?'

'Yes, sir, I…'

'The pair of you outside my office now.'

The BSM's room doubled as his office. A table and chair gave it the title.

'Tell me about it, Bombardier Nichol.'

'It was wild out there, sir. Worse than I've ever seen it, stone throwing and chanting. Taking the piss. A lad gave Thomas the 'come on' so he hit him.'

'He hit him several times?'

'Yes, sir. Until I separated them.'

'Thomas?'

'Like he said, sir. They were chanting and taking the piss about Mr Balshaw. And this kid was just asking for it so I…'

'So you put him in hospital. What the hell were you thinking?'

'I was there with Mr Balshaw, sir, and I just snapped. I know it was wrong, but…'

'You're not kidding it was wrong. The fan's spinning fast. Somehow we've got to sort this crap out.'

The anger was boiling and his manner never changed, but deep down he knew he could easily have reacted the same way at Thomas's age.

'Get away and sort you kit out.'

***

A Military Police team took statements from Nichol and all of his patrol.

An hour later the BC returned from talking to the CO. In his office were the Battery Second in Command and the BSM.

'Brigade have put out a simple statement that a soldier and a civilian were involved in an incident in Caldwell Street this afternoon and that the civilian was taken to hospital. The matter is under investigation so nothing more can be said. They hope interest will die down, but we'll have to wait and see what happens.

We failed to foresee Thomas's problem, now we've got to be aware of the mood in the rest of the battery. For this reason the CO has called a halt to all patrolling by Seventeen Battery for forty-eight hours. The other batteries will assume our responsibilities.

BSM, put Thomas in open arrest. He's to be cross-posted immediately to HQ Battery until this is all sorted out.'

They acknowledged. The BSM shook his head. After sixteen years serving with pride, mostly with Seventeen Battery, to be relieved of their duties was a personal humiliation.

***

When the Military Police report came through the CO and Adjutant went to the HQ to discuss it. Thankfully, there had been no further developments so it was decided that the CO could administer the disciplinary procedure.

The CO sat behind his desk. Standing before him was Gunner Thomas. The RSM stood close behind Thomas with the BSM on his right. The CO read out the charge.

'How do you plead?'

'Guilty, sir.'

'The evidence is documentary, contained in this Military Police report. Are you familiar with it?... Is this your signature on this statement?'

'Yes, sir.'

'Do you have anything to add?'

'Yes, sir. On the day in question there were crowds of people on the street and a lot of stone throwing. They were jeering at us, particularly the women, sir. They were singing a song about Mr Balshaw. He was a great bloke, sir. I was behind him when he was hit. It could have been me, sir. I tried to walk on, but this youth was just grinning at me and asking for it. I lost it and hit him. I know it was wrong, very wrong, sir, and I am sorry for letting the regiment down.'

'I see… Battery Sergeant Major, what is your assessment of Gunner Thomas.'

'Sir, I have known Gunner Thomas well for the six years he has been in the battery. For a year he was a member of my gun sub. He was conscientious, reliable and hard working at all times and in all weathers.

The results of the courses he has attended have been excellent. He is almost ready for promotion and until now his conduct has been exemplary. Since deploying to Belfast his performance on the streets has been excellent.

Given his close involvement with Mr Balshaw I can understand, but in no way condone, his actions. I believe he is a good man, sir, who momentarily lost control.'

'I see. Thank you, Sergeant Major… Thomas, will you accept my award or do you wish to go to Court Martial?'

'Your award, sir.'

'I've reviewed the evidence, listened to your plea in mitigation and taken note of your BSM's words.

What you did was wrong, wrong for many reasons and you know it. Our role is to maintain the law and, in that, our conduct must at all times be beyond criticism. You let the regiment down in a moment of blind fury which I cannot excuse.

However, I am aware of the enormous part that you played in the incident concerning Mr Balshaw and I note the significant impact it has had on you.

In view of that I am prepared to admonish you. I am also putting you on a three-month warning. This does not mean you are not guilty. It means 'no punishment'. If your conduct gives any rise for concern in the next three months I will have no hesitation in recommending your discharge from the army. Do I make myself clear?'

'Yes, sir.'

'Admonished. March out.'

Outside the office the RSM placed his face two inches from Thomas's nose.

'You, Gunner Thomas, are a lucky boy, a very lucky boy. Shift your arse down to the MT and get back to Seventeen Battery out of my sight. I don't want to see you again'

'Sir.'

***

When Taff arrived back he was called straight into the BSM's office.

'Listen, lad. You've been given a second chance. Put it all behind you and get back on the horse. You're going back to your old bedspace with B Section and Steve Nichol, but I don't want you on the streets yet. You're working in the 'Q' stores. There's plenty to do there, keeping the show on the road and with your energy and enthusiasm you'll make a huge difference.

I have complete faith in you.'

'Thank you, sir.'

He looked him firmly in the eye.

'And Thomas, I pushed my luck a long way with the BC and RSM to make sure you got a good hearing… Don't let me down… Now push off.'

'I won't, sir.'

***

In December the regiment returned to the UK. The month was filled with well-deserved leave and parties in every mess. With matching hangovers the chiefs wrote reports while the Indians took their artillery out of 'care and preservation'.

On 18 December the Regiment was standing down for Christmas. The Battery was mustered in the gun sheds for an address by the BC.

The BSM called the parade to attention, but, as the BC approached, the formality was lost and the Jolly Green Giant couldn't suppress a smile. On crutches alongside the BC was Lieutenant Balshaw. He proudly joined the officers on a flank and the BC began his address.

'Firstly I must thank you, every one of you, for the outstanding work you did in Ireland…

Enjoy your leave. You deserve it…

The new Year will be busy when we re-train in our artillery role…

I have no doubt you will prove, again, that you are the best gun battery in the Regiment.'

The BSM fell the parade out and they adjourned to the back of the gun shed where there was a stack of beer. He ripped out a can of Belgian lager and thrust it at Balshaw.

'Great to see you back, sir.'

'Thank you, Sergeant Major.' Grinning, he looked at the label. 'Ah "Wife Beater"! How did you know that was my favourite?'

'When do you think you'll be with us again, sir?' He smiled.

'End of March with luck, but lots of re-hab to do yet.' Sadly he knew his rugby career was over.

He quickly found Nichol and Thomas and laughed and chatted with them. With many driving off for Christmas the BSM had made sure there was only just enough beer, so the gathering soon began to disperse.

Steve Nichol looked at Taff

'When d'you start rear party, Taff?'

'Tonight at six.'

At the age of four, Taff was taken into care after his father left his mother. He had joined the army as a junior soldier at sixteen. He thrived, but he lost contact with his only brother after his second prison sentence, so the army became his family.

Taff by name only, he had no family in Wales or anywhere to call home, so he volunteered to be part of the Christmas rear party back in camp.

'What are you doing on Christmas Day? Come round to us.'

'Nah, I'll be all right, honest.'

'Don't be so daft. Mo and the boys would love to see you'. About ten o'clock, OK?'

***

Neat and deodorised, Taff rang the Nichols' doorbell on Christmas morning, a slab of 'Wife Beater' under one arm and a carrier bag of presents on the other. They had a noisy morning with the kids before Maureen did the traditional lunch. Then Steve and Taff slouched on the sofa, watching the Queen. Their eyes drooped.

In the evening they inflicted serious damage on the slab of lager in front of 'Morecombe and Wise'.

Steve and Maureen slipped off to bed and left Taff to sleep on the sofa. There had been no mention or even a thought of Ireland.

Next morning Maureen smiled at the devastation to her once beautiful lounge. Taff opened a bleary eye and swung his feet on to the floor, a vision of loveliness in Marks and Spencer's underpants. She handed him a mug of tea and a strip of paracetamol.

'Mo, you're a life saver, an absolute treasure.'

***

A few months later the Honours and Awards for Northern Ireland were released.

Bombardier Steven Nichol was awarded a Military Medal. Maureen got a new hat.

Balshaw and several others from the battery were also recognised.

After twenty-two years' service Taff Thomas left the army as a Staff Sergeant. He and the Nichol family remained lifelong friends.

He didn't let the BSM down.

31

Extreme Foraging

In the October edition of the Parish Magazine Mel wrote a delightful article about foraging that struck a chord with me. I am a lifelong forager, but not just in the sense that Mel describes. In my lifetime I have taken it to new levels.

I am a 'Baby Boomer' born when food was rationed and everything was in short supply. The enormous gardens of Fifties council houses bear witness to the fact that all families grew their own vegetables. Foraging was an essential means of supplementing our modest diet.

Blackberrying was our family's favourite activity. On one occasion, my six-foot father was reaching for, the juiciest blackberries on the highest bramble, just as Mel remembers it. He felt a sharp prick in his foot, quickly followed by a second intense stab of pain. Looking down at his sandals, he saw an adder scurrying away.

He drove like Stirling Moss to Salisbury Infirmary where he received a massive shot of anti-biotics and painkillers. He then drove us all sedately home, nursing a feeling if intense nausea and a headache that would have felled a buffalo.

Dad also followed Mel's example and spoiled 'Mother's Ruin' with sloes that he had foraged. Other wines were brewed from scratch. Rhubarb wine and potato wine came from his garden and elderberry from the hedgerow. On Monday mornings we would go to school, backs aching and fingers stained from foraging for the thousands of flower heads needed for dandelion wine.

In the spring of 1956 we picnic-ed on Salisbury Plain, surrounded by nodding cowslips. My father, my elder sister and I filled bags with them. Mother was excused picking as she was so heavily pregnant and could only sit on a rug and take off the heads. My younger sister was born that May. The wonderful, golden cowslip wine that resulted was his greatest brew and he carefully saved the last bottle to crack in celebration on her twenty-first birthday – sheer nectar.

Today cowslips are protected so this would not be possible.

The field with the best mushrooms was always a closely guarded secret. Now, sadly, weed killers have made field mushrooms a rarity and I've yet to follow the current fashion of foraging for fungi. I wouldn't want to risk a psychedelic moment at my age.

It was my mother who introduced me to advanced level foraging, extending the skills involved to other areas of life. Her foraging regularly took her to jumble sales where she would find armfuls of treasure. 'You'll grow to fit it' is a phrase that still sends shivers down my spine. Millennials should search Google for 'jumble sale'.

Newly married, I honed my urban foraging skills. Our first home was in Woolwich where stocking our larder meant foraging in the local Tesco. I was alarmed to discover that my new wife and I approached this simple task differently. We strolled the aisles together seeking offers, but she would only buy the items needed on her carefully composed list. Shopping bored me, so I would stack the trolley with bargains. If it was cheap, you bought lots and avoided shopping again for a long time. It was the start of my belief that there is more to life than the middle isle of Lidl.

When I borrowed a membership card for a local cash and carry our eyes widened at the cheap prices, so we filled our trolleys with super economy, battalion sized packs. Seduced by the absence of VAT on the labels we maxed out the Barclaycard in one swift visit.

Back home buyer's remorse set in with a vengeance as we gazed in horror at the quantity we had bought. True, we didn't need cornflakes or Andrex for many months, but in my enthusiasm we had over-purchased several items in massive quantities.

I have guilty memories of a forty-eight pack of Windolene which for many years was given generously to friends and neighbours at every opportunity. In fact, we may still have a few if anyone is interested.

Ever after, our family's weekly shop became a female sport. In forty-five years of married life, I can count on my fingers the number of times we have done the Tesco run together and it suits us both fine (I think!).

Where we did forage successfully together was at auctions. These were the days of DIY, stripped pine and Laura Ashley (yawn). With my modest wood working ability and my wife's excellent sewing and upholstery skills we made a good team.

Our pinnacle was the restoration of a drop ended settee and easy chairs. My task, securing the wooden frame etc, was straight forward, but re-upholstering became a never-ending saga.

Slaves to traditional methods and material, we needed to replace much of the original stuffing so we salvaged two smelly horse hair mattresses. The hair was soaked in the bath, sewn into pillow cases and put in the washing machine.

It was then dried, tumbled and teased-out, a process that took weeks.

The current tenants of that house are probably still digging horse hair from every plug hole. The finished product was excellent, but there was a tacit agreement that it would never be repeated.

The advent of boot fairs and eBay heralded the start of my time as an extreme forager as it provided openings to sell my better foraging bargains. It was a carousel of opportunities: buy at boot fairs and sell on eBay, buy on eBay and sell at auction, buy at auction and sell at boot fairs. It was great fun - a mildly addictive treasure hunt, always seeking the elusive find that might net a fortune.

Retirement has caused a slowdown. I gaze at the shelves in my shed, groaning with fifty years of foraged items that 'might come in handy one day', and I know that reconciliation is needed. Am I entering a de-foraging phase? Should I stop?

Just a minute, look at the time! The village shop is having a sale today. No time to waste, I must fly.

Perhaps on the way home I can forage some blackberries. Mel would approve of that.

… On Tuesday I see my therapist.

32

A Last Night of Freedom

The tiny hatch on the cell door dropped open and the duty copper peered in. Hands clasped behind his head, Stan Green stared at the ceiling. It had been a great couple of days, they'd spent a pile of money and, boy, had they shifted some beer. That Len Hooper could sure hold his ale. Len had beat it through the corridors of the four-star hotel when the police raided the bar. Stan was not so lucky.

He smiled. Tomorrow they were coming to take him back to custody in the North East. He knew the form. It didn't bother him; he'd been inside many times before. For a career criminal he'd had a singular lack of success, in fact, every step was marked with failure.

***

Tom Lyle was coming to the end of a boring shift in the CID office of the South Shields Police Station. His day had been spent trawling through endless lists of names, addresses and dates of birth, trying to find a match with the suspects they had for a current case. This was not the glamourous rogue-chasing he'd imagined plain clothes policing would be. But life stars on the bottom rung and he was easily the youngest ever to be selected for his local CID.

The Custody Sergeant stood in the door.

'Dave, I need a favour from your boys, please.'

'Sure, mate, what's the problem?'

'They've just picked up Stan Green down south and they want one of our boys to go down to Bristol and collect him tomorrow. It should be someone in plain clothes.'

'Yeah, I suppose.' Obliged the CID Sergeant. 'Tom, you can do that. It'll get you away from all those lists. Do you know Stan?'

'Sure do. We all know Stan. He was a regular customer when I was in uniform. Hauled him in pissed as a rat many a time. I took statements when he struck lucky at the Mallet's place. I wonder what he did with all that money, even he couldn't drink that much. No doubt he'd have a good go, bloody alky.' He looked at the custody Sergeant.

'OK, he's a docile old sod, not likely to cause any bother, so you're on your own. It's a good five hours each way by train. You're on allowances, should be enough to buy you a comic and a bottle of pop and don't forget the prisoner. Here's the train times. A car will pick you up at five thirty. Oh, and before you go you'll need to draw a security case. There'll be a little surprise there for you' He smiled.

***

Tom found a seat on the train, threw his 'comic', a car mag, on the seat beside him and dozed. The train pulled into Temple Meads around lunch time and a Bristol policeman drove him to the Central Police Station.

Stan was led in by a constable, clutching a shiny new sports grip and a strong box.

'Well young Mr Lyle, nice to see a friendly face again.'

'Stan you useless old git. I've wasted a valuable chunk of my life coming all this way to pick you up.'

They ticked off the list of his possessions in the grip then opened the strong box. Inside was the 'little surprise': hundreds of bank notes. They confirmed the total as £2,843. Stan smiled with pride.

'Christ, Stan, how the hell did you get as much as this?'

'Ah, Mr Lyle, it's a long tale. There'll likely be time to tell it on the train.'

***

The train pulled out with Stan in the window seat and Tom by the aisle. Soon they were heading north.

'Well Stan, looks like you're in for a lengthy stretch again. How many years have you done inside now?'

'No idea, I'm sixty-three so it must be twenty or more. I've been in and out all me life. It's all I know.'

'Why, Stan, why? There must be something better. You said you'd tell me on the train.'

'I did, didn't I?' A crafty sideways look. 'But I'll need a cup of tea to start me going.'

'OK, you old devil' He smiled and with the security case in his hand he led the way to the buffet car.

'Two teas, please.'

'A Hobnob would be nice.'

He fixed him with a scowl. 'And two packets of Hobnobs.'

Back in their seats. 'Right, then, let's hear it.'

'Well there's not much to tell, really. Never had nothing as a kid, Had to scrap for everything.'

'Why?'

'Me ma and pa were bombed out during the war so they moved in with granddad in the tenements by the docks. Dad and grandad worked in the shipyard, granny took in washing and ma had her work cut out looking after six kids.

There was never enough to go round. Anything left lying about was fair game. Thieving came naturally. We'd skive off school on the lookout for things to nick, shop lifting and the like. Juvenile court was a waste, just a slap on the wrist.

Approved school only introduced me to a crowd who were as bad as me. When I came out there was a gang of us in South Shields who'd rob anything. It was mainly garages and sheds and a bit of burglary.

A couple of short sentences then I got into bigger things, Post Office jobs and corner shops. I was usually the lookout, but I was inside one day when the manager got stroppy so one of the boys whacked him, a couple of times actually, quite hard and he almost died. I never hit him, but I got eight years.

When I got out I tried going straight, but I couldn't make it work. so I drifted back. I've been in and out of nick ever since. I don't do violence or drugs. You know my line, you've lifted me often enough, more laundromat than Brink's-Matt.

I've nothing to my name, not a bean. What I get I drink. The Sally Army feeds me sometimes. Lenny Hooper lets me doss on his settee most nights.'

Stan was an out and out rogue, but he was good company and Tom was enjoying his tales. It sure helped to pass a long journey.

'And how did you end up in trouble this time? What was that all about?'

'Well, now, I'm beginning to get a bit thirsty' I might need a little drink to help me remember that.'

'You cheeky sod. My exes cover food. Alcohol is way off limits.'

'I reckon that's my money you've got in that security case. I'm happy for you to use that.'

'Your money, dream on! You stole it.'

'Nope, not until it's proven.'

'No it's evidence. You can't tamper with evidence.'

'No one will notice a few quid. Come on, let me buy you a pint - just one? I'm in for a tidy stretch, surely you wouldn't begrudge a man a little drink on his last day of freedom?'

'Just one, OK?'

They headed for the buffet.

'Two pints of Export, please.' He put his hand discretely in the security case and took out a pound note. 'Come on, let's hear it.'

'Well me and Lenny Hooper were cruising in his transit, on the lookout, up the posh end of South Shields. We parked up and were on foot in Cavendish Avenue, big houses, high hedges – easy pickings. And we saw this young piece come rushing out with a bairn screaming. She'd left in a rush, so we went in for a look, as we thought she might have been a bit careless. Sure enough a kitchen window was on the latch.

'Yeah, that was Hayley Mallet, the owner. The kid had been ill and crying all morning and she was rushing off to the doctor's. I took her statement.'

'Anyway, no one was in so we set about gathering the electrical items. Len had the TV and microwave, cables tied, stacked by the front door ready for a quick pick up with the transit. Surprising how many people leave ready cash in a tin in a kitchen cupboard. In the unit above the kettle I found a couple of biscuit tins, both stuffed full with bank notes.'

'Her old man's a bookie. That's stuff he didn't want the taxman to know about.'

'Really? I robbed a bookie? I should get remission for that!

We forgot about the electrical stuff, shoved the loot in a Tesco bag and legged it back to the transit as casually as you can when you've just picked up several grand in readies. We drove out to the country and looked at what we had. Honest, there was more money than I'd ever seen in me life, so we split it two ways.

Your boys were gonnna guess it was us and pretty soon things would get hot. We had to bug out fast so we left the tranny in a car stack and got the first train south. It just happened to be going to Bristol, a nice, big place so we could easily get lost there.

Thirsty work all this talking… Fancy another beer?'

Tom smiled disapprovingly and reached in the security bag.

'That's kind of yeh, cheers… We had a few beers, got some new clobber from a sports store and decided to find somewhere to stay. With a Tesco bag of loot you don't do the doss houses so we found a bloody big, smart place with flunkies at the door and stuff.

We booked five nights with this stuck-up bird with stick on eye lashes at reception. Four hundred and eighty quid it was, so I give her cash. She had to call a mate over to help count it. Then she asked for me name. I had to think quick, so I said ‘Milburn… Jackie Milburn’ first name that came into me head. Len smiled and when she asked him he said ‘Robson… Bobby Robson’. Daft cow had no idea.’

The beer was going down well and Stan was warming to his story. He pushed his empty glass forward.

Then we went on a bender for three days – residents lounge every night ‘til two. We had a great time even though southern beer’s crap. By the third evening the management were starting to get a bit arsey. Two rowdy Geordies flashing wads of notes in Nike jogging suits didn’t exactly fit their four-star image.

Around midnight we were having a competition eating the olives. Too many salty olives can only end one way and Lenny threw up – a four star throw up. He fell off this big chromium bar stool and smashed a poncey glass table.

Next thing was blue lights and stab vests and I was hauled off. Lenny was in the Gents and managed to slip away. So here I am.’

Stan was in full flow, slowly, but effectively, drinking Tom under the table, determined to enjoy his last day of freedom. A couple stood next to Stan at the bar.

‘Would you like to join us for a drink?’ Without thinking Tom put his hand in the bag again.

A pair of Punks were sitting at a table: tattoos, leather, zips, chains, all the gear. One topped it with a Mohican, dyed like a rainbow.

‘You lookin’ at me? What’s your problem?’

Through the alcohol Tom braced at the challenge.

‘No problem mate, just wondering.’ Stan replied.

‘Wondering what? Didn’t you do funny things when you were young.’

‘Aye, I once screwed a parrot and I wondered of you might be my son. Wanna pint?’

‘Eat your heart out Les Dawson.’

The rest of the buffet had been watching nervously and now laughed.

‘Yeah, we both do.’ He scowled, his bravado deflated.

Tom reached into the security case and found another note.

As the train headed north more people joined the group. The singing started with Bladon Races. A rip-roaring party was developing as Tom dipped more frequently into the case. A lot of people were going to remember Stan Green’s last day of freedom.

As they drew closer to Newcastle Tom struggled to think what to do when they were met off the train. He was in trouble.

He stepped on to the platform and steadied himself. Stan was smiling and looked as right as ninepence. A policeman met them at the barrier and led them to a van. He shut the prisoner and escort in the back and wrinkled his nose. There was a strong smell of beer. Surely not?

The Custody Sergeant and a young PC stood ready to receive Stan. The CID Sergeant was behind them.

‘Name.’

‘Jackie Milburn.’ Laughed Stan unsteadily.

‘OK, Stan, you can cut that out.’

They completed the rest of the Custody Register. Stan's sports grip was tipped on the table and the contents logged. Then, the security bag was opened and the money was carefully counted. Tom flinched when he realised how much smaller it had become. His only hope was that there was no cross-reference with Bristol over the sum he'd received.

Stan was led away. 'So long, folks. See ya another day, Mr Lyle.'

'No chance.' Tom replied.

The CID Sergeant looked at Tom, stone faced. 'The driver will take you home, Tom. I want to see you at 9am tomorrow outside the DCI's office. Got it?'

'Got it, Sarge.'

A clean shave and a crisp shirt couldn't disguise Tom's hangover. There was a lot of shouting and finger wagging from the Detective Chief Inspector, but thankfully no disciplinary entry on his records. A sly old lag had made a fool of him and it was a lesson he'd never forget.

Down in the cells Stan's eyes were closed. His head was thumping like Charlie Watts's base drum, but he didn't care. As a last night of freedom that would be a hard act to beat.

33

Pining For Christmas

Many people have a special place, somewhere they can relax and think. Mine is a bench on Ham Common overlooking Poole Harbour. I always pause there to take in the view to the Islands and the distant hills of Purbeck.

It was early December and the day was bright and clear with no one to bother me or the dog. I sat on the bench enjoying the fresh winter breezes.

'A great day.' A voice said.

I was watching a windsurfer, bouncing across the waves in the winter chill. 'Yes, fantastic. Just look at that view.'

'Yeah. What ya thinking?'

Wind surfing in winter is a hard way to get your kicks, but it fills you with exhilaration and a zest for life. This guy was roaring along.

'Counting my blessings, really. I've led a full and satisfying life. I've travelled with a wife of nearly fifty years who's shared the thrills and spills along the way. I have two sons and five lovely grand-daughters to enjoy my retirement with. There are just the aches and pains that come with advancing years. With family and friends, a life well-lived and still much to come, I'm a lucky man. And you?

'I'm a lot younger than you, but I don't get around much. I'm not bothered, my two sisters and my parents are nearby. Gran and grandad are not far away. Grandad lost a limb in the storm last year, but they get along fine.'

I was still watching the wind surfer, braced against the wind. In a few minutes he would be back ashore skin stinging from the salt and the cold, heart pumping, a hundred per cent alive. I was once like that.

I looked up and turned round to see who I had been talking to, but there was no one there. I peered left and right along the track, but it was empty.

'What's the matter? Can't you see me?'

I was all alone. Was it a trick of some sort? Was someone hiding?

'OK, well done. You had me fooled. You can come out now.'

'I'm here, right here in front of you.'

I looked down.

'Theres nothing here just a few pine trees.'

'That's it. Got it in one.'

'Eh?'

'Three feet in front of your left knee, the pine sapling, that's me.'

'What?' I scratched my head, still looking cautiously around. 'I can't have been talking to a tree. That's ridiculous.'

'You have, mate. Just like Prince Charles and he did OK.'

'King Charles' I corrected.

'Whatever. No one's laughing now. People listen these days when he talks about the environment. I've seen you here before haven't I?'

'Have you?'

‘Yes, I wouldn’t forget that dog of yours. Nasty little beast peed on my friend over there.’

‘Oh, I’m sorry.’

‘That’s OK. I suppose it’s what dogs do.’

‘Yes and I suppose it’s what trees are for.’

‘You what? No one has the right to behave like that towards others, particularly my friends. It’s disgraceful’

‘No, no, of course not. How long have you been here?’

‘I’m five and my sisters just here are eight and ten. Mum and dad, across the path are in their forties and gran and granddad by the lake are nearly a hundred and fifty. That’s granddad’s limb by grandma’s foot. The tree surgeon did a good job.’

‘Do you like it here?’

‘Yeah, it’s all right, but I get a bit down as Christmas approaches.’

‘That’s not unusual, lots of folk hate the short dark days. Doctors have a name for it.’

‘Yes, but it’s worse for us. We always lose a few family members around now. It’ll be my cousin this year.’

‘Really?’

‘Yes, a few years ago his mother’s fir cones were all taken by a nurseryman from the New Forest. He and his brothers were raised in a polytunnel and when they were seedlings they were taken out and planted in lines all exactly two metres apart. Row upon neat row, thousands of them in soulless blocks. Just like living in Stevenage. That’s no way to grow up and now Christmas is coming.’

‘No, I hate forestry blocks too.’

‘He’s fifteen so this’ll be his last year.’

‘Why so?’

‘Oh come on, Christmas – holly and mistletoe and…?’

‘A Christmas tree!’

‘That dreadful word! I can’t bring myself to say it. At least holly grows back, but for my cousin with no roots it’s the end.’

‘Yes, but…’ I struggled to find the words. ‘Yes, but think of the happiness he will give to everyone. A Chr… uh, a tree brightens the house at Christmas and brings joy to us all. Those synthetic lavatory brush trees just don’t cut it.’

‘Then he’s off to recycling – no dignity. We’re just not valued.’

‘No, you’re wrong. We all love trees. They give us so much. Like people, they achieve different things and some live longer lives than others.

‘Whatever.’

I was a woodworker and have a passion for wood. My son makes beautiful furniture and shares my enthusiasm. He’s a chip off the old block. Oh, I’m sorry, no offence intended.’

‘None taken.’

‘Wood is tactile and has so many different characteristics. Each tree has its own appeal, the strength of oak, the warmth of cherry, the silkiness of walnut, creamy sycamore and yew with its wonderful tangled grain.

It’s *your* heritage. You’re from the great Pinaceae family. Yours is not the glory of fine furniture, but things like fence posts and telegraph poles, the basics of life that we simply couldn't live without. We must also remember the environment.'

'Oh no, not the King again.'

'Yes, the King, he has always emphasised the enormous value of trees. They enhance the landscape and provide beautiful recreation spaces for us to enjoy. Trees host a myriad of insects and encourage birds to feed in their branches. The carbon dioxide that we breathe out, that so harms the planet, nourishes trees and they give back oxygen which sustains us.'

'Whatever. Unlike that mangey mutt of yours. Carbon dioxide comes out of one end and methane out of the other. Bloody oxygen thief, cows aren't all to blame you know.'

'Just leave him out of it. He's my pal.' The dog growled menacingly.

'Keep him under control.'

'Yes, OK. Different roles mean different life spans for trees, but in any role their importance is as great. We can't live without you. Sadly your cousin will not enjoy a long life, but at Christmas he will be the centre of the festivities. He'll bring joy and happiness and will *make* Christmas for some lucky family.'

'Whatever.'

'If you spend the rest of your life here and grow tall like your parents you will be a key part of a beautiful place and if your roots grow deep, who knows, *you* may play an important role in protecting the coast of Poole harbour from sea erosion.

Life treats us all differently, my young friend, and it often seems unfair, but we are all of equal importance. Be sad at the loss of your cousin, but be pleased that he will make a family very happy at Christmas.'

'I've never thought of it like that. That's amazing. Thank you.'

'It's getting late. I must be going.'

'Will you be back again? I've enjoyed our chat.'

'Yes, certainly, and for many years to come, I hope. It's my favourite place. Besides, I'm looking forward to enjoying the summer shade that you and your sisters will provide when you're bigger. Just don't tell my friends I've been talking to trees.'

'I won't, but remember, it did no harm to Charles. See ya some time.'

***

It was dark when I reached home and my wife was busying herself around the kitchen.

'You're late.' She smiled. 'Had a good walk? What kept you?'

'Yes, excellent. I've been talking to uh… an old friend. And you?'

'Oh, starting to get things set for Christmas. We must go and buy a tree tomorrow. It's never Christmas without a proper tree. A tree always makes Christmas.'

I smiled, 'Yes, it certainly does.'

34

My Guilty Secret

I have a dark secret that has long been gnawing at my mind.

I have always mocked those who enclose a Christmas letter with their card. You know the sort, an exercise in the banal, written in the third person.

> *'... In February Marjorie painted the kitchen. She chose magnolia again as it matched her complexion, In July Gerald had a new set of dentures, so much better than the old ones...'*

My secret is that, since 2003, I too have written a Christmas letter and I've compounded the felony by keeping copies of all of them all.

There, I've said it. I feel so much better now.

Browsing through the collection I realised that they provide a fascinating record of how our family has developed over the years. They now sit in a 'memory box', poorly hidden, for my sons to find when I turn my toes up.

One edition in particular is interesting. The 2020 letter was the year of the Covid lock down and will perhaps show future generations how we coped living through such unusual times. I've reproduced it here:

THE BOLDNGREY CHRISTMAS LETTER 2020

This remarkable year has provided me with the challenge of writing a thousand words about nothing. Regular readers may think little has changed!

It began so well in January when we had a very pleasant reunion with most of my cousins on my mother's side. I treated them to a cripplingly cold tour of the many family graves in Shrewton Church Yard. Afterwards a cousin provided lunch in her home, followed by photographs and family memories.

In February I had my left hip replaced. All went to plan and I was briefly able to leap tall building again, that is, until the Government Lockdown put them out of bounds.

In response to warnings and TV pictures of panic buying, Barbara bought three packets of pasta and a twin pack of Andrex. Covid measures meant that I had to cancel my last year's Christmas present of tickets for the Mayflower Theatre in Southampton.

We soon settled into a routine which didn't trouble me too much, breakfast, long walk with the dog then into the shed making things, tidying and throwing away items that for twenty-five years I had been keeping 'just in case they came in useful'. Coping with boredom is a military skill that I have retained.

With more clubs and societies than me, life was more difficult for Barbara. For her it was breakfast, followed by a massive clean and tidy of the house and garden then a long walk with the dog and into her sewing room.

After six weeks I had a life time's stock of craft items to sell and had revealed areas of my shed floor that I hadn't seen since the Queen's Coronation. With no craft fairs and, most of all, no rugby, days lost their identity and Mondays ran in to Sundays without variation.

The house and garden were now spotlessly tidy and there were forty-two miles of bunting piled neatly in the sewing room. My socks were perfectly ironed, my boxer shorts had knife edge creases down the front and Barbara was seeking a lock up in which to store the quantity of jams, chutneys and sloe gin(!) that she made from the bumper fruit crop. She completed slightly more laps of the garden than Captain Tom Moore, but sadly her sponsorship money barely covered the cost of the grass seed needed to re-turf the lawn. All the while, the dog hid under the table, paws blistered, limbs aching, desperately hoping that another walk was not in the offing. Every so often we saw the grand-children through the window as they passed.

The boys and their families coped well. John worked from home and home-schooled his two, with assistance from Joe Wicks. The government's emphasis on cycling defined Philip as a key worker. Cycling boomed and he has never been so busy.

On 15 June lockdown was lifted with half a pack of pasta remaining and no requirement for torn copies of the Daily Mirror in the loo. We re-booked the tickets for the Mayflower and I narrowly avoided needing a general anaesthetic for my post-covid haircut.

Strangely enough I never realised that Barbara was a food fascist, but throughout lockdown she closely supervised my calorie intake. Whether it was the diet or the haircut I lost well over a stone, but I'm working on picking the combination lock that she fitted to the larder door.

Our aim was always to lead life as normally as possible within the constraints of the pandemic, so routine activities became major events.

We managed covid compliant pub lunches for our birthdays, but perhaps the happiest day of the summer was when all the families were able to celebrate the twins' sixth birthday, paddle boarding at Studland. It was so enjoyable that no one noticed that it was one of the few days this summer when it howled with rain!

With the autumn lockdown, we had a better idea of what to expect and settled into the old routine.

Remember, remember the Fourth of November… As a boy I would make a huge bonfire with a Guy in our garden, always on the Fifth of November. It was something that I tried to do with our sons as they grew up, though garden bonfires have since become problematic.

Fireworks are now a family tradition which the grandchildren look forward to with great excitement. With lockdown starting on the fifth of November, Bonfire Night on the fourth became a glorious pre-lockdown family party. Those four bright, excited, happy little faces with cocoa and Barbie-burgers are a memory that will last long after Covid is forgotten.

Again we cancelled my Christmas present tickets for the Mayflower Theatre, but this time we were able to 'bubble' with the twins and resume happy child care duties.

Like many, we have sadly lost friends to the virus but we know that 2020 has been kinder to our family than many others. It's just a lost year at a time in life when every day counts, but we can look forward to 2021 with hope. Who knows, I may get to use my tickets for the Mayflower at last, but best of all there will be a new grandchild in the spring.

No prizes for guessing what some people did during lockdown!

Dear Santa, please bring us all a Covid vaccine for Christmas.

Wishing you all a happy and healthy Christmas from Boldngrey and Family

PS: For sale: 2020 Year Planner – unused.

35

Malcolm and Doreen's Christmas Letter

Earlier in the book I introduced you to Malcolm and Doreen who met through a pensioners' portal on a dating site. That happened a few years ago and marked the start of a relationship that has led to a very happy marriage.

We have become firm friends and I thought you might be interested in the letter that Doreen recently enclosed with her Christmas card.

MALCOLM AND DOREEN'S CHRISTMAS LETTER 2023

Well, what a year, where do we start? January seems a good place (ha ha) when Malcolm had his first cold of the year and had to take to his bed for two days. How grateful he was for those lovely warm bed socks that I knitted for him last Christmas.

In February it was very cold. I expect it was for you as well, so Malcolm decided to re-do the bathroom.

We were all surprised in March when Malcolm's teenage niece, Peaches, decided she was going to call herself Willow and change her pronouns to he/him/they. I was never much good at English so I don't really understand. Malcolm said that we shouldn't call him 'Willy', but I think that was one of his little jokes.

April was my birthday and Malcolm surprised me with a lovely new colander. How he noticed the plastic one that mother gave me was beginning to show signs of wear I'll never know. He's so attentive. Chrome this time, very adventurous and all a bit 'Jamie Oliver'.

In spring Willow decided to change back to Peaches again. It seems she didn't go much on being a boy, which I can quite understand. Now she says she's 'non-binary'. Does that mean two school uniforms? More expense, I suppose.

We were very upset when the Queen died last year. We all thought she was really lovely, but it looks like things will turn out OK with Charles, though Malcolm is a bit worried about the corgis. He says Andrew is not a fit person to look after them. I don't know. I never did understand quite what he did.

We loved the Coronation, especially the horses and Camilla. We watched it all on the BBC (well Malcolm did nod off at about four). Huw Edwards did such a lovely job, but we don't seem to see much of him these days. Malcolm said he's probably with Andrew and the corgis.

Malcolm had a big birthday in July. I can't say, but it was between sixty-nine and seventy-one (ha ha). Malcolm's younger brother Darren and his wife Sharon arranged a lovely party at the Eventide Centre. They're, such a nice couple and Sharon does a lovely lemon drizzle. Malcolm said 'No candles or we'll have to call the Fire Brigade'. He's a one.

Malcolm, as always, wore the tie clip and cuff links he was given by his gran for his twenty-first birthday all those years ago and Mavis-next-door made a lovely job of my perm. It was a lovely day and Malcolm was so happy with the lovely Val Doonican box set that I bought as his present. Bless him.

Darren and Sharon's family are well. Harper, Darren's eldest girl, has just split from her third partner. Her new man is Erroll. He seems a lovely boy and is so good with all of Harper's children. We do hope it will last, although he does have a court appearance in the New Year.

Brooklyn, their boy, was a bit disappointed as he wanted to join the Army this year, but apparently they're keen on education these days and wouldn't let him in as some of his tattoos were spelt wrong. His little sister, Boscombe, has now turned seventeen and is looking forward to her first tattoo. Potty training for Grayson, their youngest, is coming on well and they hope he will be dry by the time he starts Senior School.

Peaches? I think she or he or they are now 'gender fluid'. These teenagers, I think I understood it when they were just gay.

We booked a coach trip to Torquay again for our summer holiday in August. It's our fifth year at Reg and Lily's B and B. They're are such a lovely couple and always do a lovely roast. The trip was a bit disappointing as the coach driver did rather spoil it for us. Poor Malcolm is a martyr to his prostate and these days needs more and more comfort stops, but there was no need for the driver to be so impatient and rude, especially when the motorway policeman had been so understanding. Anyway, Malcolm's seen the doc and hopes to get done in 2025.

Peaches says that they are now 'trans-gender', something else Malcolm and I don't understand. She was such lovely people; we just can't keep up. It could be worse though. Their best friend has self-identified as a cat. What does that do to school uniform?

We both love Christmas, so in October Malcolm put the tree up, nothing like being ready in good time. Malcolm's eight-foot inflatable snowman looks lovely out the front again, but this year he had to buy some stronger string to tie it up, as last year it blew down the street and got stuck in the Co-op doorway. He's also added a ten-foot Santa and sleigh. Rudolph's nose lights up just like real – it looks lovely.

We're at Darren and Sharon's for the big day as usual. It's so nice there and Sharon does a lovely brandy butter, but it does sound funny to think we're going to watch the King's Speech.

Well, Malcom's already bought a lovely 'Birds of Britain 2024 Calendar' so we're all set up for the New Year and we will have something to look forward to as Malcolm has almost finished re-decorating the bathroom. The tiling is fairly straight and it looks…

So that was our year.

Hoping you all have a Merry Christmas
and a Lovely New Year

Love from

Malcolm and Doreen XXX

36

Growing Old

I am now well into the fourth quarter of my life and recently had a recurrence of my heart problems. I have sadly become aware that I wear my dark suit more often for funerals than for weddings. Perhaps it's time to put my life in some sort of order, to consider the things that I've done and what might lie ahead.

Bill McKenna wrote:

> *Life is not a journey to the grave with the intention of arriving safely in one pretty and preserved piece, but to slide across the line broadside, thoroughly used up, worn out, leaking oil, shouting GERONIMO!*

That sums me up and although I've been leaking oil for some time, I'm not yet ready for the big slide. I can safely say that as an arthritic cardiac patient with a prostate problem I am *enjoying* the *worst* of health, frustrated by a twenty-year-old mind struggling inside a body with ninety-year-old joints.

I still suffer anxieties, but they are in check and are generally related to age and infirmity rather than traumatic events. I can comfortably read and recall military accounts which I would previously have found harrowing. I can choose to do what *I* want to do and to give in to my long-held phobias and obsessive traits, *if I need to*, without a sense of guilt.

I can withdraw into my shed and use my time, retirement's most precious asset, to indulge my hobbies or just potter around. I can sit and think, or just sit… I can take exercise, walk the dog to the limits of *our* arthritis and enjoy that same blue sky that I so loved as a boy.

When it gets dark, I come indoors and search the internet for lost relatives, ever broadening my knowledge of my ancestors. I use my woodworking skills to make items that *I* want to make and I can extend my love for wood to the furniture at Kingston Lacy, where I am a National Trust volunteer.

My rugby boots still lie, mud encrusted, somewhere in the back of the wardrobe, never officially hung up, but my interest in Rugby is still very much alive as a fan. I no longer have a season ticket for Bath, but remain staunchly one-eyed in my support. I can also enjoy club rugby at Swanage and Wareham, played in the spirit and style that I so valued in my playing days, even though for several years my youngest son has been officially a 'veteran'. I might add, the only veteran whose mother still comes to watch him play.

What of my relationship with Murphy and his law? While I was drafting this piece I woke one morning feeling anxious, for no apparent reason. That evening we were going to the theatre, but, other than that, I had nothing unusual planned. So I told myself to stop worrying, as nothing was going to happen, and felt better as the day wore on.

Walking from the car to the theatre, a bus approached so we stopped at the kerb. As it passed, I felt a blow to my forehead and I realised that I had been struck by a wing mirror. It pulled up at a stop and I approached the driver. As I took my hat off, blood poured down my face from a cut to my forehead.

Someone called an ambulance and I was treated on the spot. Fortunately it didn't require stitching, but the delay meant that the pleasant Thai meal before the show was replaced by hasty junk-burger and my wife had the embarrassment of visiting the theatre in the company of an elderly gent with blood encrusted eyebrows and a headache that would have felled a horse.

That morning I felt something might go wrong, but to suggest that I would be run over by a bus would have been just stupid, wouldn't it? I think I can safely say my relationship with Murphy is as strong as ever, which probably means that I will not die in my sleep!

I have always considered myself a Christian, despite the fact that I am only an occasional churchgoer. I believe being a Christian is much about the way in which you lead your life and, if I didn't do so well in my youth, I have tried to live my later years in a more Christian manner. I wonder what comes next? I suppose I believe in some sort of afterlife. Certainly, I've always wanted to see my mum again, but how will she recognise me as I was only fourteen when she died?

These days it seems almost obligatory to acknowledge our past misdemeanours and our guilt, so should I say 'sorry' to those I have hurt or upset along the way? Perhaps, in this age of recycling, I should start by apologising to the organ donor organisations as, approaching the line broadside and leaking oil, there can be little left of my body that is worth passing on. I have always maintained that it's better to wear out than rust out so, sadly, few of my organs would benefit anyone.

My many encounters with the medical profession have left me with a replacement knee and two hips and various stents, staples, screws and plates, but have solved the problem of what to do with my body when I die. There's no need for cremation or burial, just wheel me down to the scrap merchant and weigh me in

With age is supposed to come wisdom and I suppose I must reluctantly accept that it would be foolish to ride a bicycle again after I had been drinking.

My wife has loyally stood by me all this time and remains my life partner. We have an increasing band of grandchildren, the first of whom was born on 29th February

2012, thus perpetuating my theory that the unusual happens to my family.

I love them all dearly and am immensely proud of them, so what words of wisdom could I offer?

My old friend Kipling gave wise advice in 'If', but I would begin by saying, 'Never forget that kindness is the most important virtue because unless you treat people with kindness you have no right to expect kindness in return and without kindness none of the other virtues is possible.'

Secondly, as Mark Twain almost said, 'Twenty years from now you will be more disappointed by the things that you didn't do than the things you did', so 'Carpe Diem!'

But they have been born into a hard world and they will need guidance. They will need someone to set them on a path through life that avoids its many pitfalls.

Most importantly, they will need someone to help them to distinguish between mischief and trouble in the hope that at some time in the distant future they too will achieve that glorious broadside slide across the line.

That person could be me.

GERONIMO!

Meet The Author

Like Boldngrey, Harry Beaves is a baby boomer. He was born 'at home' in a Police Station in Savernake Forest where his father was the village policeman.

He attended Bishop Wordsworth's School at the time when William Golding taught English there. Some may consider him one of 'Scruff' Golding's failures!

He was commissioned from Sandhurst into the Royal Artillery in 1968 and looked forward to an energetic and exciting military career. Garison life in Cold War Germany in his first posting was dull and boring and failed to live up to expectation until his regiment undertook an emergency tour in one of the most difficult areas of Northern Ireland in 1972.

Subsequent jobs as an army commando and in service adventure training satisfied his quest for adventure. His active and energetic military career of 34 years was without the need for significant financial outlay on promotion parties.

A triple heart by-pass at the age of 47 was a major reason for his leaving the army. He retrained as a furniture maker winning a City and Guilds Gold Medal for Cabinet making. This became his employment until retirement.

For more than thirty years he had kept the experiences of 1972 battened down in his memory. Without the invisible support of the military network they came crashing to the fore and he suffered seriously from Post Traumatic Stress Disorder.

It took a long time to regain some sort of normality and in 2018, in part as a cathartic exercise, he wrote his autobiography:

'Down Among the Weeds'
(ISBN 9781788037532)

In doing so he discovered a love for writing which has led to this anthology.

Printed in Great Britain
by Amazon

61905664R00122